The Mountain Walker's Guide to Wales

THE MOUNTAIN WALKER'S GUIDE TO WALES

Colin Adams

Gwasg Carreg Gwalch

ISBN: 0-86381-154-X

Map by Ken Gruffydd

First published in 1990 by Gwasg Carreg Gwalch,
Capel Garmon, Llanrwst, Gwynedd,
Wales.
Tel: 06902 261

CONTENTS

The Routes

MOELWYNI

RHINOG

ARENNIG

BERWYN

ARAN

CADAIR IDRIS

DYFI FOREST

PUMLUMON

ACKNOWLEDGEMENTS

The author wishes to thank the staff of the Royal Commission on Ancient and Historical Monuments in Wales, Aberystwyth, for providing invaluable information during the preparation of this book. He is also grateful to the organisations and individuals who have given their advice and assistance. For their specific help, particular thanks must go to the following: the Central Electricity Generating Board; the Forestry Commission; Gwynedd County Council; the Nature Conservancy Council; the Ramblers' Association; and the Severn-Trent and Welsh Water Authorities; Sandra Owen of Cwm y Glo near Caernarfon, who had attained every conceivable mountain summit in the Principality before her twenty-first birthday; Edna Wood of Trefor near Caernarfon; Connie Hollingworth of Vaynol Park near Bangor; Peter Crew of the Snowdonia National Park; Hywel Jones of Carmel near Holywell; Elwyn Edwards of Bala; Howard Williams of the Brecon Beacons National Park; and Peter Morgan Jones of Tredegar.

Colin Adams, a former Army physical training instructor, has considerable mountain walking experience in Britain, Germany, Norway and South Yemen. His first taste of walking in Snowdonia came as a sixteen-year-old apprentice during a course at the Army Outward Bound School in Tywyn. It was during an SAS selection course at Hereford four years later that he first encountered the mountains of South Wales. Since then he has made thousands of climbs to mountain summits all over Wales. He has reached the remote Carneddau summit of Creigiau Gleision over 400 times.

INTRODUCTION

The main purpose of this guide is to benefit, irrespective of age or experience, those who enjoy mountain walking in Wales. It may also be useful or of interest to any visitor to Wales. The guide is unique and comprehensive. Its framework is based on common sense and simplicity. Incorporated in 100 routes, the guide brings together all the Principality's notable mountain groups and covers every significant mountain summit within them except the few where there are problems concerning access. Twenty groups and 200 summits are covered. The main objective of each route is to attain at least one summit. The book is suitable for every category of walker. Some of the excursions are strenuous, requiring a high level of fitness and a sound knowledge of mountaincraft; many will suit novices seeking to widen their horizons; and others have in mind casual walkers and family groups.

The Mountain Groups

The twenty groups have been arranged in the guide starting in the north-west corner of the Principality and finishing in the south-east. To avoid any confusion between the Black Mountains and the Black Mountain (Mynydd Du), the latter has been referred to by its local name, Carmarthen Fan. The groups, in book order, are as follows:

Llŷn	an ancient Celtic stronghold
Eifionydd	intriguing hills where history and legend blend
Snowdon	the pride of Wales and the land of King Arthur
Glyder	a textbook example of a landscape created by glaciers
Carneddau	contains the largest area of land above 1000m in the British Isles outside Scotland
Clwydian	modest hills, witness to a turbulent past

Moelwyni	the industrial dereliction is now a part of the heritage of Gwynedd
Rhinog	provides some of the most rugged and demanding walking in Britain
Arennig	lonely peaks rise above abandoned valleys
Berwyn	possesses its own brand of beauty
Aran	a fascinating place but access is restricted
Cadair Idris	savage country
Dyfi Forest	an area of unbroken solitude, vast skies and broad expanses
Pumlumon	high windswept moorland, solemn and mysterious
Cwmdeuddwr	Wales's great wilderness
Radnor Forest	a jewel in the British countryside
Carmarthen Fan	a fastness to be reckoned with
Fforest Fawr	an ancient hunting ground, unforgettable territory
Brecon Beacons	South Wales's principal mountain group
Black Mountains	superb ridge walking country

The Routes

The explicit style of the 100 route descriptions has eliminated the need for maps or sketches throughout the guide. Information about each route, in the order in which it is given, is as follows:
summary Immediately beneath the route number, the summary provides an idea as to the walk's severity and points out any special difficulties. It may also suggest the category of walker to whom it is best suited. No attempt, however, has been made to define these categories. Precisely what is a novice walker, for example, is debatable. Likewise, an experienced walker, a casual walker, cannot be effectively categorised. Nor can the walks themselves be meaningfully classified. A number of factors, such as different weather conditions, mean that systems of grading mountains walks can only be vague and liable to misinterpretation. Generally speaking, though not always, the longer the walk the more demanding it is.

group The mountain group in which the walk takes place.

number of summits The number of mountain summits the walk attains. (Outlying summits have been incorporated in the nearest group.)

time required The time given is for the complete walk, there and back, but excludes any for pauses in progress such as rest periods. The times are based on a walking speed of 4km per hour, with one minute added for each 10m of ascent. They are to the nearest fifteen minutes. An allowance, ranging from fifteen to forty-five minutes, has been included in the times given where routes cross a particularly severe terrain. No allowance, however, has been made for descending since on the average journey the reduced speed caused by the sharp slopes, will normally be cancelled out by that gained on the gentle ones. Nor has an allowance been made for the weight of any load carried as this will vary considerably, depending on the route and the walker. A heavy load will obviously reduce progress appreciably.

map The number is given of the Ordnance Survey map sheet on which the route is based. The Outdoor Leisure Series have been used in the areas covered by them, otherwise the Landranger Series. Each route has been carefully planned to start and finish at the same point and to require the use of only one sheet. Throughout the guide the spelling of Welsh place names may vary insignificantly from those on the map.

start The start of the walk, chosen with safe car parking in mind, is shown by a six-figure grid reference and named. As stated previously, all walks finish at this point.

parking Always at or close to the start of the walk and chosen where possible in unconcealed locations, not always the most convenient but those considered to be the safest. Nevertheless, the usual precautions regarding the safety of parked vehicles should be taken.

nearest centre The nearest place to the start of the walk where the following facilities can be found: accommodation, bank, cafe, garage, post office, shops and toilets. The distance to it is also given. The place stated, of course, is not always the nearest to where some of these facilities can be found.

summit details Their number, as specified in the Table (see p.19), name, height in metres, grid reference, characteristics and other information.

route description A clear and concise description enabling the walker to follow the route with little or no reference to the map. Changes of detail will inevitably occur in the course of time but are unlikely to render the description sufficiently inaccurate as to mislead those following it. Descriptions are related where possible to detail least likely to change. Modern cairns, in particular, appear and disappear more readily than most landmarks and no important reference has been made to them. References to the points of the compass are approximate.

associated route features Absorbing facts on such are given where appropriate.

Access

Most of the routes are over public rights of way leading to open country where the public has a legal right of access. Of those that are not, every effort has been made to ensure that access to them is currently acceptable but, of course, this cannot be guaranteed. Generally speaking, even where no rights exist, most landowners throughout Wales are happy to allow walkers who observe the Country Code to cross their property, especially with prior consultation.

The Country Code drawn up by the Countryside Commission

★ guard against all risks of fire
★ fasten all gates unless you are sure they should be open
★ keep dogs under proper control
★ keep to paths across all farmland
★ avoid damaging fences, hedges and walls
★ leave livestock, crops and machinery alone
★ leave no litter
★ help to keep all water clean
★ protect wildlife, plants and trees
★ drive and walk carefully on country roads
★ make no unnecessary noise
★ respect the countryside and the way of life of those who live there

Winter

In winter conditions, many of the routes in this guide require technical competence and should only be attempted by those both suitably experienced and properly equipped. Winter transforms the hills into possible death-traps. Even the walks to the low altitude summits can become entirely different propositions.

SAFETY AND EQUIPMENT

Because the routes in this guide range from easy strolls to demanding high level excursions, clothing and equipment needs will vary considerably. Requirements will also depend, of course, on the season in which a walk is undertaken. For the simple walks (Route 8, for example), the only essential items during the summer months are stout shoes and a showerproof anorak or jacket. Being properly kitted out is an important aspect to safety but, regarding the exact items, it is very much a personal matter. Always prepare pessimistically for the weather, even when the forecast is favourable. For the moderate trips (Route 7, for example), walking boots, a windproof anorak, a waterproof cagoule, walking breeches or thick trousers (not jeans), a map and compass, together with a rucksack containing a spare jumper, food and drink, are essential. Rucksacks are seldom waterproof and a thick plastic bag should be used as an inner liner. On all routes where the time given is three hours or more, clothing and equipment must include, in addition to the above (Route 7), overtrousers, gaiters, woollen stockings (two pairs are often worn), a hat or balaclava, waxed wool or leather gloves, spare emergency clothing, a first aid kit, a torch, a whistle and a survival bag for each person. Survival bags should be made of heavy-duty polythene, large enough to cover the whole body and brightly coloured so as to be picked out easily at a distance. A survival bag can save a life.

The Basic Guidelines of Mountain Safety

★ make sure that the walk chosen is well within the capabilities of each member of the party
★ plan walks with a reasonable time allowance
★ check the local weather forecast before leaving
★ leave written word of your intended route, keep to it and report back on return
★ make sure that all clothing and equipment fits comfortably and is in good condition
★ walk at a pace that suits the slowest member of the party
★ ensure that the party always stay together and that nobody becomes detached from it

* never venture into mountainous areas alone unless sufficiently confident and experienced
* always trust the compass — it is easy to become disorientated and believe it is wrong (a Silva compass is recommended and will not require a protractor and ruler when in use)
* know first aid and the signs of heat disorders and frostbite
* do not hesitate to retreat to lower ground or turn back if weather conditions deteriorate
* after every stop on route, check to see that nothing is mislaid
* remember that the final descent at the end of the day is often the most hazardous part of the walk

Notes on Scrambling

* do not crowd each other on the rocks
* check where the feet are placed
* keep hand holds low and stand away from the rock
* test each hold
* keep heels down
* keep three points of the body in contact with the rock
* if a rock is dislodged shout 'below'

Emergencies

In the event of an accident or illness within the party, get to the nearest mountain rescue post or telephone. Dial 999 and ask for the police. Leave one of the party with the patient if numbers permit. When it is not possible to summon help, the international mountain distress signal can be given. The signal is six blasts on a whistle (or six shouts or flashes of a torch) followed by a minute's silence, then repeated as necessary. The reply is three such blasts/shouts/flashes repeated at minute intervals.

TABLE OF THE TWENTY MOUNTAIN GROUPS COVERED IN THIS GUIDE, SHOWING THE DISTRIBUTION OF THE 100 ROUTES AND 200 MOUNTAIN SUMMITS

	Number of Routes	*Number of Summits*
Llŷn	2	6
Eifionydd	6	12
Snowdon	5	11
Glyder	5	11
Carneddau	8	25
Clwydian	4	6
Moelwyni	7	16
Rhinog	6	9
Arennig	7	9
Berwyn	7	13
Aran	1	2
Cadair Idris	3	7
Dyfi Forest	4	8
Pumlumon	3	6
Cwmdeuddwr	3	4
Radnor Forest	2	5
Carmarthen Fan	4	10
Fforest Fawr	5	8
Brecon Beacons	6	12
Black Mountains	12	20

MAP SHOWING WHERE THE MOUNTAIN GROUPS ARE LOCATED

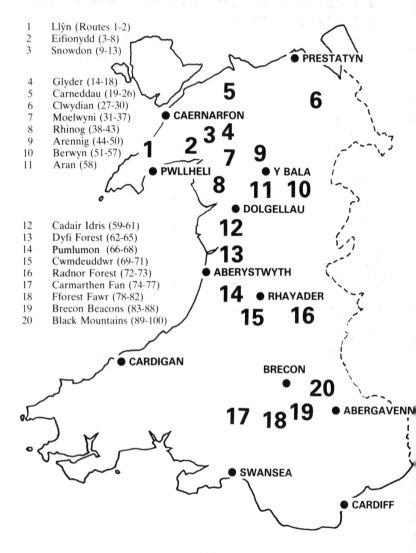

1   Llŷn (Routes 1-2)
2   Eifionydd (3-8)
3   Snowdon (9-13)

4   Glyder (14-18)
5   Carneddau (19-26)
6   Clwydian (27-30)
7   Moelwyni (31-37)
8   Rhinog (38-43)
9   Arennig (44-50)
10   Berwyn (51-57)
11   Aran (58)

12   Cadair Idris (59-61)
13   Dyfi Forest (62-65)
14   Pumlumon (66-68)
15   Cwmdeuddwr (69-71)
16   Radnor Forest (72-73)
17   Carmarthen Fan (74-77)
18   Fforest Fawr (78-82)
19   Brecon Beacons (83-88)
20   Black Mountains (89-100)

TABLE OF MOUNTAIN SUMMITS COVERED IN THIS GUIDE ARRANGED IN ORDER OF ALTITUDE IN METRES, SHOWING THEIR MOUNTAIN GROUP

1	Yr Wyddfa (Snowdon)	1085	Snowdon
2	Crib y Ddysgl	1065	Snowdon
3	Carnedd Llywelyn	1064	Carneddau
4	Carnedd Dafydd	1044	Carneddau
5	Glyder Fawr	999	Glyder
6	Glyder Fach	994	Glyder
7	Pen yr Ole Wen	978	Carneddau
8	Foel Grach	976	Carneddau
9	Yr Elen	962	Carneddau
10	Y Garn	947	Glyder
11	Foel Fras	942	Carneddau
12	Garnedd Uchaf	926	Carneddau
13	Elidir Fawr	924	Glyder
14	Y Grib Goch	923	Snowdon
15	Tryfan	915	Glyder
16	Aran Fawddwy	905	Aran
17	Y Lliwedd	898	Snowdon
18	Pen y Gadair	893	Cadair Idris
19	Pen y Fan	886	Brecon Beacons
20	Aran Benllyn	885	Aran
21	Corn Du	873	Brecon Beacons
22	Moel Siabod	872	Moelwyni
23	Mynydd Moel	863	Cadair Idris
24	Arennig Fawr	854	Arennig
25	Llwytmor	849	Carneddau
26	Pen yr Helgi Du	833	Carneddau
27	Foel Goch	831	Glyder
28	Cadair Berwyn	830	Berwyn
29	Moel Sych	827	Berwyn
30	Carnedd y Filiast	822	Glyder
31	Mynydd Perfedd	812	Glyder
32	Cyfrwy	811	Cadair Idris
33	Waun Fach	810	Black Mountains

34	Bera Bach	807	Carneddau
35	Y Foel Goch	805	Glyder
36	Fan Brycheiniog	802	Carmarthen Fan
37	Pen y Gadair Fawr	800	Black Mountains
38	Penllithrig-y-wrach	799	Carneddau
39	Cribyn	795	Brecon Beacons
40	Bera Mawr	794	Carneddau
41	Mynydd Pencoed	791	Cadair Idris
42	Cadair Fronwen	785	Berwyn
43	Moel Hebog	782	Eifionydd
44	Drum	770	Carneddau
45	Moelwyn Mawr	770	Moelwyni
46	Waun Rydd	769	Brecon Beacons
47	Gallt yr Ogof	763	Glyder
48	Fan Hir	760	Carmarthen Fan
49	Drosgl	758	Carneddau
50	Y Llethr	756	Rhinog
51	Pen Pumlumon Fawr	752	Pumlumon
52	Moel Llyfnant	751	Arennig
53	Diffwys	750	Rhinog
54	Bannau Shir Gâr	749	Carmarthen Fan
55	Y Aran	747	Snowdon
56	Tomle	742	Berwyn
57	Pen Pumlumon Arwystli	741	Pumlumon
58	Craig Cwm Silyn	734	Eifionydd
59	Fan Fawr	734	Fforest Fawr
60	Rhobell Fawr	734	Arennig
61	Gwaun Cerrig Llwydion	730	Brecon Beacons
62	Pen Pumlumon Llygad Bychan	727	Pumlumon
63	Moel Eilio	726	Snowdon
64	Fan Gyhirych	725	Fforest Fawr
65	Rhinog Fawr	720	Rhinog
66	Fan y Big	719	Brecon Beacons
67	Pen Allt Mawr	719	Black Mountains
68	Pen Rhos Dirion	713	Black Mountains
69	Rhinog Fach	712	Rhinog
70	Moelwyn Bach	710	Moelwyni
71	Trum y Ddysgl	709	Eifionydd
72	Pen Cerrig Calch	701	Black Mountains
73	Garnedd Goch	700	Eifionydd

74	Allt Fawr	698	Moelwyni
75	Mynydd Mawr	698	Eifionydd
76	Mynydd Drws y Coed	695	Eifionydd
77	Foel Wen	691	Berwyn
78	Twmpa	690	Black Mountains
79	Arennig Fach	689	Arennig
80	Cnicht	689	Moelwyni
81	Y Garn	684	Pumlumon
82	Gau Graig	683	Cadair Idris
83	Mynydd Tarw	681	Berwyn
84	Chwarel y Fan	679	Black Mountains
85	Creigiau Gleision	678	Carneddau
86	Hay Bluff	677	Black Mountains
87	Moel Druman	676	Moelwyni
88	Maesglasau	674	Dyfi Forest
89	Moel Cynghorion	674	Snowdon
90	Ysgafell Wen (South)	672	Moelwyni
91	Waun Oer	670	Dyfi Forest
92	Carnedd y Filiast	669	Arennig
93	Ysgafell Wen (North)	669	Moelwyni
94	Cyrniau Nod	667	Berwyn
95	Tarren y Gesail	667	Dyfi Forest
96	Fan Nedd	663	Fforest Fawr
97	Mynydd Llysiau	663	Black Mountains
98	Y Dduallt	662	Arennig
99	Manod Mawr (South)	661	Moelwyni
100	Tyrau Mawr	661	Cadair Idris
101	Great Rhos	660	Radnor Forest
102	Cribin Fawr	659	Dyfi Forest
103	Manod Mawr (North)	658	Moelwyni
104	Pen Twyn Mawr	658	Black Mountains
105	Moel yr Ogof	655	Eifionydd
106	Allt Lwyd	654	Brecon Beacons
107	Mynydd Talymignedd	653	Eifionydd
108	Black Mixen	650	Radnor Forest
109	Foel Cwm Sian Lwyd	648	Berwyn
110	Moel yr Hydd	648	Moelwyni
111	Pen Twyn Glas	646	Black Mountains
112	Drygarn Fawr	645	Cwmdeuddwr
113	Carnedd Llechwedd Llyfn	643	Arennig

114	Moel Lefn	638	Eifionydd
115	Garreg Las	635	Carmarthen Fan
116	Pen Cowlyd	634	Carneddau
117	Tarren Hendre	634	Dyfi Forest
118	Y Garn	633	Eifionydd
119	Fan Llia	632	Fforest Fawr
120	Moel Fferna	630	Berwyn
121	Stac Rhos	630	Berwyn
122	Craig Cerrig Gleisiad	629	Fforest Fawr
123	Fan Frynych	629	Fforest Fawr
124	Foel Gron	629	Snowdon
125	Y Garn	629	Rhinog
126	Foel y Geifr	626	Berwyn
127	Moel y Cerrig Duon	625	Berwyn
128	Moel Penamnen	623	Moelwyni
129	Moel Ysgafarnogod	623	Rhinog
130	Pen y Castell	623	Carneddau
131	Craig y Llyn	622	Cadair Idris
132	Foel Boeth	619	Arennig
133	Gallt y Wenallt	619	Snowdon
134	Garreg Lwyd	619	Carmarthen Fan
135	Y Gurn	619	Brecon Beacons
136	Cefn yr Ystrad	617	Brecon Beacons
137	Fan Dringarth	617	Fforest Fawr
138	Cefn Gwyntog	615	Berwyn
139	Gorllwyn	613	Cwmdeuddwr
140	Foel Goch	611	Arennig
141	Bache Hill	610	Radnor Forest
142	Tal y Fan	610	Carneddau
143	Mynydd Craig Goch	609	Eifionydd
144	Mynydd Troed	609	Black Mountains
145	Moel Meirch	607	Moelwyni
146	Foel Goch	605	Snowdon
147	Mynydd Ceiswyn	605	Dyfi Forest
148	Mynydd Dolgoed	605	Dyfi Forest
149	Y Gamriw	604	Cwmdeuddwr
150	Foel Lwyd	603	Carneddau
151	Foel Fraith	602	Carmarthen Fan
152	Whimble	599	Radnor Forest
153	Clip	596	Rhinog

154	Mynydd Pen y Fal	596	Black Mountains
155	Carnedd y Cribau	591	Moelwyni
156	Moel Feity	591	Carmarthen Fan
157	Yr Arddu	589	Moelwyni
158	Moelfre	588	Rhinog
159	Carreg yr Ogof	585	Carmarthen Fan
160	Moel Wnion	580	Carneddau
161	Moel Farlwyd	577	Moelwyni
162	Drybedd	566	Pumlumon
163	Pant y Creigiau	565	Brecon Beacons
164	Yr Eifl (Central)	564	Llŷn
165	Bryn	562	Brecon Beacons
166	Blorenge	561	Black Mountains
167	Cefn y Cylchau	556	Carmarthen Fan
168	Moel Fama	555	Clwydian
169	Tor y Foel	551	Brecon Beacons
170	Crug Mawr	550	Black Mountains
171	Craig Wen	548	Carneddau
172	Y Gurn	542	Carneddau
173	Drum Ddu	537	Cwmdeuddwr
174	Moel y Griafolen	535	Rhinog
175	Y Gurn Ddu	522	Llŷn
176	Mynydd Llan-gors	515	Black Mountains
177	Foel Fenlli	511	Clwydian
178	Bwlch Mawr	509	Llŷn
179	Disgwylfa Fawr	507	Pumlumon
180	Cowlod	502	Radnor Forest
181	Y Gurn Goch	492	Llŷn
182	Mynydd Tan y Coed	491	Dyfi Forest
183	Ysgyryd Fawr	486	Black Mountains
184	Yr Eifl (Tre'r Ceiri)	485	Llŷn
185	Crimpiau	475	Carneddau
186	Moel Dywyll	475	Clwydian
187	Y Garn Wen	471	Black Mountains
188	Moel Arthur	455	Clwydian
189	Crug Hywel	451	Black Mountains
190	Yr Eifl (North)	444	Llŷn
191	Cefn Du	441	Snowdon
192	Pen y Cloddiau	439	Clwydian
193	Moelfre	435	Carneddau

194	Moel Tryfan	427	Eifionydd
195	Foel Darw	424	Carmarthen Fan
196	Moel Plas-yw	419	Clwydian
197	Moelyci	410	Glyder
198	Moel Faban	409	Carneddau
199	Bryn Arw	384	Black Mountains
200	Twyn y Gaer	367	Fforest Fawr

ROUTE 1

A stirring walk on secret hills. Can be attempted by fit family groups.

Group	Llŷn
Number of summits	3
Time required	2¾ hours
Map	O.S. 1:50 000 Landranger Sheet 123
Start	At 352440 — the former Forestry Commission car park
Parking	Car park at the start
Nearest centre	Pwllheli (11km)

1st Summit   **190 YR EIFL (NORTH)**
444m   **360457**
Carries an ancient burial cairn.

2nd Summit   **164 YR EIFL (CENTRAL)**
564m   **364447**
Carries an ancient burial cairn surmounted by a trig pillar.

3rd Summit   **184 YR EIFL (TRE'R CEIRI)**
485m   **374447**
Carries an ancient burial cairn probably of Bronze Age origin, suggesting that the area was inhabited long before the existence of Tre'r Ceiri (Town of the Giants), the famous Celtic settlement by which name the hill is always known. The 2ha oval settlement stronghold, protected by multivallate defences, supports the tumbled relics of over 100 stone dwellings, variously proportioned and probably once roofed with timber and bracken. The Town of the Giants, the most impressive Iron Age monument in Wales, appears to have been founded shortly before the Roman invasion of Britain (see p.74) and remained in use throughout their three and a half centuries of military occupation.

From the car park, cross the road to the track, turn left and ascend to the head of the pass, Bwlch yr Eifl. Pass through the fence gate onto the quarry track (once providing access to the upper banks of Eifl Quarry),* bear left at the fork and climb sharply to the first summit, Yr Eifl (North). Go back through the gate, pass beneath the power lines and progress along the steepening path. After 250m, cross the traversing path and press on upslope to the summit of the central peak. Drop down south-east to the wall, pass through the gap and turn right. On reaching the stile, turn left onto the path, pass through the 'High Street' of the Town of the Giants and proceed to the third and final summit cairn.

To return, go back along the path, go over the stile crossing the wall and continue forward. Take the path to the homestead, Gors Lwyd (not named on the map), turn right onto the track and follow the wall back to the car park.

* Eifl Quarry, for a century or more the mainstay of Trefor village, was first worked for stone on a large scale in 1850 by the Welsh Granite Company. Three years earlier, their owners, Hutton and Roscoe, had purchased the nearby Gwylwyr Quarry from Samuel Holland (slate magnate, elected Liberal MP for Merioneth in 1870). About 1843, Holland took an interest in sett-making, buying the Gwylwyr Quarry with the intention of supplying the stone for the construction of the planned new harbour at Porth Dinllaen. However, when Holyhead was chosen as the main link with Ireland, Holland lost interest, selling his concern to Hutton and Roscoe. In 1918, the Eifl Quarry was taken over by the Penmaenmawr and North Wales Granite Company, employing at its zenith in 1925, over 700 men. It closed in 1967.

ROUTE 2

A taste of remoteness without venturing far from civilisation. Not for the beginner.

Group	Llŷn
Number of summits	3
Time required	4 hours
Map	O.S. 1:50 000 Landranger Sheet 123
Start	At 414496 — Clynnog Fawr Church*
Parking	Limited roadside in the village
Nearest centre	Caernarfon (16km)

1st Summit   178 BWLCH MAWR
509m   **426478**
Carries a trig pillar.

2nd Summit 175 Y GURN DDU
522m   **401467**
One of the great summit viewpoints of Wales. The highest point is marked by a cairn.

3rd Summit 181 Y GURN GOCH
492m   **407475**
Marked by a cairn.

Opposite the church lych-gate, pass the post office and follow the lane until 25m past the cattle grid. Then mount the seldom-used path, ignoring the track, ascend through the bracken and progress to the farmhouse, Pen yr Allt Isaf (not named on the map). Pass through the gates, follow the track to the upper farmhouse (Pen yr Allt Uchaf) and pass beneath the power lines. Continue along the track and after about 600m, pass through the wall gate, bear a shade left and make headway upslope where, in time, beyond the rock bluffs, a wall comes into view and a complex wall system is encountered. At the dip in the wall, cross the stile to the first summit, Bwlch Mawr. From here, recross the stile, drop down south-west to the wall corner and head upslope with the wall to the left. Where the wall turns left, bear left and after 400m, at the junction near two large cairns (primitive burial monuments), cross the boulder in the wall and bear right to Y Gurn Ddu, the second summit. Descend north-east to the wall and continue forward beside the rising wall to the third summit, Y Gurn Goch.

To return, head just north of east and drop down sharply to the far corner of the forest. Turn left beside the perimeter wall, pass through the gate and walk back to the village.

* Clynnog Fawr Church, cathedral-like in atmosphere, was built in the sixteenth century, dedicated to St Beuno. It is best known for its magnificent late-Perpendicular windows. A noteworthy relic in the north transept is the huge strong-box, hollowed out of a single block of oak, known as 'Cyff Beuno' (Beuno's Chest). Hailed the St David of North Wales, Beuno came to Clynnog Fawr in 616 and founded a monastery here on land given to him by Cadwallon ap Cadfan, King of Gwynedd, in return for a golden sceptre. Half a millennium later, the monastery destroyed by war, a small teaching church was built near the ruins. It developed into a rare non-tribal collegiate portionary church (a mother church where the portionists — honorary canons — were resident). St Beuno's shrine chapel was built about 1540, soon after the present church to which it is connected by a passage from the tower. The chapel is said to be directly above Beuno's burial place, but his remains have never been discovered.

ROUTE 3

Provides a remarkable variation of scenery. For experienced walkers.

Group	Eifionydd
Number of summits	3
Time required	4½ hours
Map	O.S. 1:25 000 Outdoor Leisure Sheet 17
Start	At 588481 — Beddgelert car park
Parking	Car park at the start (fee July-August)
Nearest centre	Beddgelert

1st Summit **43 MOEL HEBOG**
782m   **564469**
The watchtower of Beddgelert. Carries an ancient burial cairn surmounted by a trig pillar.

2nd Summit **105 MOEL YR OGOF**
655m   **556478**
The Hill of the Cave is named from the cave on its eastern flank where Owain ap Gruffudd Vychan, better known as Owain Glyndŵr* (anglicised by Shakespeare as Owen Glendower), is once believed to have sought refuge.

3rd Summit **114 MOEL LEFN**
638m   **553485**
Marked by a cairn.

From the car park entrance, turn right towards the Royal Goat Hotel,** take the path through the housing estate and cross the bridge and the stile. Turn right onto the path, cross the stile and turn left onto the lane. Pass through the pine wood, cross the stile next to the barn and follow the path up the mountainside. The path eventually mounts a scree-covered bluff, emerges by a key cairn and bends left to the first summit, Moel Hebog. From here, head north-west and drop down sharply beside the wall to the pass, Bwlch Meillionen. Where the wall turns left, continue forward and follow the rising path to Moel yr Ogof, the second summit. Then follow the path along the ridge crest to Moel Lefn, the third and final summit.

To return, head just south of east and descend between the outcropping rock to the forest edge. Pass through the wall gap, cross the stile in the fence and drop down to the track. Turn left and in due course, pass the vehicle barrier, bear left onto the access road and at the T-junction, turn right. After about 500m, turn left onto the narrow path which leads to another access road, turn right and cross the bridge spanning the stream, the Afon Meillionen. Turn left onto the path, continue beside the stream and turn left onto the track. Pass through the Forestry Commission campsite, turn right onto the A4085 and walk back to Beddgelert.

* Owain Glyndŵr, self-styled Prince of Wales, was born in 1354 at Sycharth in the Tanat Valley. The immortal statesman, a descendant of Bleddyn ap Cynfyn, Prince of Powys at the time of the Norman conquest of England, bravely set about obtaining independence for Wales and reversing the triumphs of Edward I. Glyndŵr's rebellion, which had strong support from the people, began when his forces attacked Ruthin in September 1400, on the eve of the fair of St Matthew. Flint, Hawarden and Rhuddlan met the same fate and in early 1401, as the uprising spread south, the great Cistercian house of Abbey Cwm-hir was sacked because the abbot supported the English. Some abbeys, however, including Strata Florida, the 'Westminster Abbey' of Wales, backed Glyndŵr and indeed John ap Hywel, abbot of Llantarnam, died fighting for him. Parliaments were held at Machynlleth and Dolgellau and alliances were sought with the French, Irish and the Scots. By 1404, the famous fortresses of Aberystwyth, Cricieth and Harlech had been captured and the presence of Glyndŵr's army was felt throughout the whole of Wales. During the next year or two, however, the tide began to turn — the young and talented Prince Henry of Monmouth, son of Henry IV (Bolingbroke), steadily restored power. By 1409, the rebellion was over and two years later, Owain mysteriously vanished, taking with him the hopes of a nation. When, where and how he died is unknown. In March 1413, Prince Henry succeeded his father as Henry V.

** The Royal Goat Hotel, an old coaching house, has offered first class accommodation to travellers since the reign of George

III. Originally named the Beddgelert Hotel, its distinguished guests included George Borrow and The Revd W. Bingley. It was later renamed the Goat Hotel and later still, after visits by Prince Arthur (Queen Victoria's third son), the Royal Goat.

ROUTE 4

A stint on the Nantlle Ridge. Can be attempted by fit novice walkers.

Group	Eifionydd
Number of summits	2
Time required	3½ hours
Map	O.S. 1:25 000 Outdoor Leisure Sheet 17
Start	At 479505 — Nebo Post Office
Parking	Limited roadside in the village
Nearest centre	Caernarfon (13km)

1st Summit **73 GARNEDD GOCH**
700m   **511495**
Carries an ancient burial cairn surmounted by a trig pillar.

2nd Summit **58 CRAIG CWM SILYN**
734m   **525502**
Carries an ancient burial cairn mutilated by the incorporation of a rudimentary shelter.

From the post office, take the lane leading east (Ffordd Cors y Llyn) and at the end, follow the track beside the wall. Pass through the gate, bear left to the wall corner and head upslope beside the wall. Where the wall turns left, continue forward, press on upslope to the next wall and turn left to the first summit, Garnedd Goch. Cross the stile, follow the path beside the wall and after 900m, at the junction, go over the stile in the fence and through the gap in the wall. The path, clearly defined, rises gently along the ridge crest, passes two square-based cairns and leads to the second summit, Craig Cwm Silyn.

Return by the same route.

ROUTE 5

A mountain walker's Utopia; the best of the Nantlle Ridge. One section of mild scrambling.

Group	Eifionydd
Number of summits	4
Time required	3¾ hours
Map	O.S. 1:25 000 Outdoor Leisure Sheet 17
Start	At 571525 — Rhyd-ddu car park
Parking	Car park at the start
Nearest centre	Beddgelert (5km)

1st Summit 118 Y GARN
633m   551526
Carries two ancient burial cairns.

2nd Summit 76 MYNYDD DRWS Y COED
695m   548518
The highest point, just south of the stile, is unmarked.

3rd Summit 71 TRUM Y DDYSGL
709m   544516
Unmarked.

4th Summit 107 MYNYDD TALYMIGNEDD
653m   535514
Carries an imposing pyramidical column, built about 1870 by the owner of Talymignedd Farm to mark the meeting place of three farm boundaries. The summit is one of the few vantage-points where the great stone fortifications of Caernarfon, Cricieth and Harlech can be seen in unison — a reminder of Gwynedd's tempestuous past.

Opposite the car park, take the slate paved path and cross the second bridge spanning the river, the Afon Gwyrfai (a main feeder of Llyn Cwellyn). Bear left onto the track, continue to the road and pass through the gate. Follow the path beside the wall, cross the bridge and the stiles and press on upslope. Traverse the boulder field to the wall, cross the stile and continue forward to the first summit, Y Garn. Head south to the wall, mount the rocky shoulder and scramble to the top where the ridge path is firmly established. Cross the stile at the second summit, Mynydd Drws y Coed, follow the path and after 500m, where the path bends left, leave it in favour of the summit it avoids, Trum y Ddysgl. Head south-west, rejoin the path and cross the narrow saddle to the unmistakable fourth and final summit, Mynydd Talymignedd.

Return by the same route, skirting the summits.

ROUTE 6

A look at the Elephant Mountain. In mist, the proficient use of map and compass will be essential.

Group	Eifionydd
Number of summits	1
Time required	2½ hours
Map	O.S. 1:25 000 Outdoor Leisure Sheet 17
Start	At 508548 — Cesarea Chapel, Y Fron
Parking	Ample roadside in the village
Nearest centre	Caernarfon (10km)

The Summit 75 MYNYDD MAWR
698m   **539546**

Known locally as the Elephant Mountain because of the strange profile it presents to the north. The summit, the centre of the 'elephant's back', carries an ancient burial cairn mutilated by the incorporation of a shelter.

From the chapel, take the road leading east (Lôn Cwm) and after 300m, turn left onto the lane which slowly degenerates into a track. Pass through the gate to the derelict cottage, bear right and drop down along the path to the tarn, Llyn Ffynhonnau, where the path ends. Keep the tarn to the right, continue forward and climb to the summit.

Return by the same route.

ROUTE 7

Attains the westernmost 600m summit in Wales. Not for the beginner.

Group	Eifionydd
Number of summits	1
Time required	2¼ hours
Map	O.S. 1:25 000 Outdoor Leisure Sheet 17
Start	At 479505 — Nebo Post Office
Parking	Limited roadside in the village
Nearest centre	Caernarfon (13km)

The Summit 143 MYNYDD CRAIG GOCH
609m   497485
A bleak and crenellated outpost. The highest point is unmarked and difficult to define.

From the post office, take the lane by the war memorial (Ffordd y Llyn) and after 700m, where the lane turns right, follow the track and pass beneath the power lines. Pass through the wall gate, keep the reservoir to the left and cross the stile. Turn right, ascend beside the fence and after about 250m, bear left where, in time, the grass gives way to rocks. On reaching the wall, pass through one of the gaps to emerge at the summit.

Return by the same route.

ROUTE 8

An escape from the summer rush. Suitable for any able-bodied person. Safe for families with young children.

Group	Eifionydd
Number of summits	1
Time required	¾ hour
Map	O.S. 1:25 000 Outdoor Leisure Sheet 17
Start	At 506567 — the road junction near Moel Tryfan Cemetery, Rhosgadfan
Parking	Ample roadside at the junction
Nearest centre	Caernarfon (8km)

The Summit 194 MOEL TRYFAN
427m   **515561**
Carries a trig pillar.

From the junction, follow the road to the right of the cemetery and at the end, turn left beside the wall. After 100m, where the wall turns left, continue forward and ascend to the summit.

Return by the same route.

ROUTE 9

An incomparable traverse of the famous Snowdon Horseshoe's most inflexible 'nails'. To be attempted only by experienced walkers familiar with exposed rock scrambling.

Group	Snowdon
Number of summits	3
Time required	5 hours
Map	O.S. 1:25 000 Outdoor Leisure Sheet 17
Start	At 647556 — Pen y Pass car park
Parking	Car park at the start (fee)
Nearest centre	Llanberis (8km)

1st Summit   14 Y GRIB GOCH
923m   **624551**

The mountain walker's ultimate conquest. The breathtaking ridge, menacingly exposed throughout, commands the utmost respect.

2nd Summit   2 CRIB Y DDYSGL
1065m   **610551**

Usually known by its ridge name rather than Carnedd Ugain, the highest point, where there is a trig pillar.

3rd Summit   1 YR WYDDFA (SNOWDON)
1085m   **609543**

The monarch of them all. One of the most frequently climbed mountains in the world and the highest in the British Isles outside Scotland. The panorama from the summit is perhaps more extensive than imagined. On a clear day it is possible to see far into four countries — Wales, England, Ireland and Scotland. Facilities at the station, the upper terminus of the Snowdon Mountain Railway,* are open only when the railway is operating. They include a souvenir shop, a cafeteria and a licensed bar. Legend has it that the summit is the burial place of the boulder-throwing giant, Rhita Fawr, who clothed himself in the beards of the kings he intimidated, including those of Nyniaw and Peibiaw. Rhita was eventually killed by King Arthur, whose grave is traditionally linked to the nearby saddle of Bwlch y Saethau, the scene of his final battle in the sixth century.

From the west corner of the car park, mount the Pig Track** and follow it as far as the pass, Bwlch y Moch, where the south side of the Horseshoe comes into view. Then head due west, follow the path to Y Grib Goch's east ridge and scramble the trail of boot-smoothed rock. On gaining the unique summit ridge, with an immense abyss to the right, keep a shade to the south of the crest and traverse about 130m to the small summit cairn. Traverse further along the ridge, resist the temptation to stray from the crest and pass the two pinnacles by dropping down to the left a shade and skirting below them (although the second is often scrambled directly over). Descend to the col, Bwlch Coch, continue along the crest to the unmistakable perpendicular slabs and drop down to the left to pass them. Regain the now broader crest, keep to the main ridge path and ascend along the Ddysgl stretch of the Horseshoe to Carnedd Ugain. From here, the path descends south-west to Bwlch Glas and the track of the mountain railway. Pass the Pig Track monolithic marker, note its location and ascend to Yr Wyddfa along the path which follows the ridge crest to the left of the railway.

To return, go back to the monolith, turn right onto the Pig Track and drop down sharply into upper Cwm Dyli. Where the track contours left near a prominent striated boulder, continue down to Glaslyn's shore and follow the Miners' Track (see p.42) back to the car park.

* The Snowdon Mountain Railway, constructed in just thirteen months along the route of an old pony path, opened in April 1896. Britain's only public rack and pinion railway, it continues to be one of the most popular tourist attractions of Wales, operating from Easter to well into the autumn, weather permitting. The 7½km journey from Llanberis to the summit station, an ascent of about 960m, takes roughly one hour.

** The Pig Track, carefully reinforced in recent years, takes its name from the pass it crosses, Bwlch y Moch (Pass of the Pigs). It is sometimes written Pyg Track, a spelling introduced by early climbers who named the track after the initials of the nearby Pen y Gwryd Hotel (see p.88).

ROUTE 10

Unveils the Horseshoe's full magnificence. For experienced walkers.

Group	Snowdon
Number of summits	2
Time required	4¼ hours
Map	O.S. 1:25 000 Outdoor Leisure Sheet 17
Start	At 647556 — Pen y Pass car park
Parking	Car park at the start (fee)
Nearest centre	Llanberis (8km)

1st Summit   **17 Y LLIWEDD**
898m   **622533**

A formidable precipice. The great cathedrals of rock plunge sensationally from the crest described as providing 'one of the finest ridge walks in Europe'.

2nd Summit   **133 GALLT Y WENALLT**
619m   **642532**

An 'end nail' in the Horseshoe. Marked by a cairn.

From the south side of the car park, take the Miners' Track* and follow it until approaching the second lake, Llyn Llydaw. Bear left at the fork, pass the valve house (associated with the CEGB's oldest power station, Cwm Dyli) and continue along the path which eventually crosses the face of a terraced rock wall. At the key cairn above, bear right at the fork, mount the jagged shoulder and ascend sharply to the top of the satellite elevation, Lliwedd Bach. Then traverse the acclaimed ridge crest to the twin peaks of Y Lliwedd, the westernmost being the higher. Go back to the key cairn, turn right and follow the tenuous path along the rarely trodden stretch of the Horseshoe to Gallt y Wenallt, the second summit.

To return, go back to the cairn, drop down to the Miners' Track and walk back to the car park.

* The Miners' Track, once known as the Gorphwysfa** Path, was constructed in the early nineteenth century to bring copper ore down from the Brittania Mine. It now serves as a popular route to Yr Wyddfa, characterised by the relics of a bygone age: the ore-crushing mill, built in 1898; the Llyn Llydaw Causeway, first crossed in 1853; and the miners' lodging barracks which convey a reassuring influence upon those perplexed by modern times.

** The Gorphwysfa was originally a small coaching inn, built at the top of Llanberis Pass near the spot now occupied by the youth hostel. The inn was opened about 1850 following the construction of a narrow road through the pass. It was later renamed the Pen y Pass Hotel. At the turn of the century, the hotel was modernised and extended and it reverted to the earlier name, the Gorphwysfa. In 1967, it was purchased by the Youth Hostel Association and extensively converted. The hostel was opened in 1971 and is the second highest in Wales.

ROUTE 11

Scales one of Snowdonia's most distinctive peaks. Can be attempted by fit novice walkers. Beware of the unfenced mine shaft.

Group	Snowdon
Number of summits	1
Time required	3¼ hours
Map	O.S. 1:25 000 Outdoor Leisure Sheet 17
Start	At 627506 — Pont Bethania car park
Parking	Car park at the start
Nearest centre	Beddgelert (5km)

The Summit 55 YR ARAN
      747m   **604515**
      Marked by a cairn.

To the south of the car park, cross the cattle grid onto the Watkin Path,* bear left at the fork and pass through the gate. Pass through the next gate to enter the nature reserve** and continue beside the cascading river, the Afon Cwm Llan. On reaching level ground and about 70m short of the bridge, turn left onto the rising path and cross the old tramway (once associated with Hafod y Llan Slate Quarry which closed about 1880). The path winds its way over grass, crosses a scree-covered slope and passes close to the unfenced mine shaft. At this point, continue forward for 200m, turn right beside the wall and higher up, cross the stile to the summit.

Return by the same route.

* The Watkin Path is the most arduous of the six main routes to Yr Wyddfa. The higher stretch, beyond Hafod y Llan Slate Quarry, was built in the late nineteenth century as a donkey path by the railway pioneer, Sir Edward Watkin, whose home nearby was known as the Chalet. The path was officially opened in September 1892 by William Ewart Gladstone, the eighty-three-year-old Prime Minister, who, two months earlier, had formed his fourth administration. (Sir Edward once made an attempt to

construct a Channel Tunnel but was opposed by the government because of military considerations. It offered a gateway to a determined invader.)

** Yr Wyddfa: Snowdon National Nature Reserve, the largest in Wales, was established in 1966 and covers a unique area of rugged mountainous country. The higher cliffs provide a refuge for carrion crows, choughs, ravens and ring ouzels. (Chough now exist in only a few places in Britain and at a distance can be mistaken for crow or jackdaw.)

ROUTE 12

A circuit of Snowdon's less familiar 'horseshoe'. For experienced walkers.

Group	Snowdon
Number of summits	4
Time required	5¼ hours
Map	O.S. 1:25 000 Outdoor Leisure Sheet 17
Start	At 580601 — Oriel Eryri car park, Llanberis
Parking	Car park at the start
Nearest centre	Llanberis

1st Summit **63 MOEL EILIO** 556577
726m
Carries an ancient burial cairn mutilated by the construction of a rudimentary shelter.

2nd Summit **124 FOEL GRON** 560568
629m
The highest point is unmarked.

3rd Summit **146 FOEL GOCH** 570563
605m
The highest point, to the north-east of the fence junction and stiles, is unmarked.

4th Summit **89 MOEL CYNGHORION** 586563
674m
The Hill of the Counsellors may once have been a political meeting place for the Druids. the obscure 'priests' of the Celts. The flat grassy summit is a splendid vantage-point for Clogwyn Du'r Arddu.*

From the car park, go to the High Street onto Capel Coch Road and progress past the farmhouse, Hafod Lydan. Where the road turns left, cross the stiles, follow the track and 50m short of the wall, turn left onto the path. Pass through the gate, continue along the path and approaching the lake, bear right to the wall.

Ascend sharply to the ridge crest, turn left at the junction and cross the stile. Then make the long traverse to Moel Eilio, the first summit. From here, head south-east to the wall gap, follow the path and drop down to the col, Bwlch Cwm Cesig. The path climbs the precipitous head of Cwm Dwythwch to the second summit, Foel Gron, crosses a cairn-marked spur and descends to another col. Ascend to the third summit, Foel Goch, cross the stile ahead and bear right. Drop down beside the fence to the pass, Bwlch Maesgwm, go over the stile next to the gate and turn left to the fourth and final summit, Moel Cynghorion.

To return, head roughly north-west and drop down sharply to the derelict farmhouse, Helfa Fain. Cross the slab spanning the stream, pass through the gates and follow the path. Go over the stile crossing the fence, pass the cottage and go over the stile crossing the wall. Turn right onto the track, continue to the stiles crossed previously and walk back to the car park.

* Clogwyn Du'r Arddu, the subject of a complete book, *The Black Cliff*, is the most daunting rock-climbing precipice in Wales. Ascended by The Revd W. Bingley in 1798, its buttresses, gullies and terraces have developed the skills and talents of many famous climbers. The cliff's dark north-facing aspect provides a suitable microclimate for arctic-alpine plants, including the rare Snowdon Lily (*Lloydia serotina*). Flowering briefly in June, the Snowdon Lily was first recorded in the seventeenth century by the Welsh botanist and scholar, Edward Lloyd.

ROUTE 13

A leisurely ramble much of which is along a metalled surface but with virtually no traffic.

Group	Snowdon
Number of summits	1
Time required	1¾ hours
Map	O.S. 1:25 000 Outdoor Leisure Sheet 17
Start	At 526600 — Groeslon crossroads
Parking	Limited roadside in the hamlet
Nearest centre	Caernarfon (5km)

The Summit 191 CEFN DU
441m   549603
Carries a trig pillar and a cairn. The site of Guglielmo Marconi's historic wireless station.*

From the crossroads, take the road leading east and cross the cattle grid to the corner of the coniferous block. At this point, bear left off the road, follow the path and traverse the gentle heather slope. After about 500m, turn left to the fence corner and continue upslope to the summit.

Return by the same route.

* The station, built at a cost of £50 000, was commissioned in March 1914 and later that year, transmitted the first direct transatlantic radio message. Marconi had first succeeded in transmitting a signal across the Atlantic in 1901 from Poldhu in Cornwall. In September 1918, the station transmitted the first direct message to Australia. During the Great War, it had been used by the Post Office and the Admiralty. It closed in 1939, although part of it was used during the Second World War as a military listening post. Remnants of the station still exist including the aerial mast support blocks, sections of steel hawsers and the trenches where the co-axial cables were run to each mast. (In 1946, Marconi became part of English Electrics which was taken over in 1969 by the electronics giant GEC.)

ROUTE 14

Spotlights the popular Cwm Idwal National Nature Reserve, * *the first in Wales. For experienced walkers.*

Group	Glyder
Number of summits	2
Time required	3½ hours
Map	O.S. 1:25 000 Outdoor Leisure Sheet 17
Start	At 649603 — Ogwen car park
Parking	Car park at the start (further facilities east along the A5)
Nearest centre	Bethesda (7km)

1st Summit 5 GLYDER FAWR
999m 642579
The highest point, unmarked, is generally acknowledged as the conspicuous rock pile with an upright slab at its southern end.

2nd Summit 6 GLYDER FACH
994m 656582
Here the highest point is in no doubt, being the top of the enormous boulder heap which conjures up images of fighting dinosaurs. The Cantilever Slab, mounted by Thomas Pennant in 1781, is one of Snowdonia's most photographed mountain features.

Go to the rear of the car park toilet block, take the path signed 'Llyn Idwal' and cross one of the stiles and the bridge. Continue along the path and pass through the fence gate to enter the nature reserve. Then bear left along Idwal's shore where presently the fine architecture of the Idwal Slabs will be recognised. The path rises, crosses a tumbling stream and leads to the rock fall below the cleft, Twll Du. Ascend to the foot of the cleft, bear left and continue upslope beside the base of the cliffs. Approaching the tarn, Llyn y Cŵn, bear left to the scree slope, pick up the cairned path and ascend to Glyder Fawr, the first summit. Head east along the path, bear right to circumvent the rock spires of Castell y Gwynt (Castle of the Winds) and scramble to the top of the second summit, the Glyder Fach boulder heap.

To return, rejoin the path, continue east and pass the Cantilever Slab. After 150m, bear left at the fork and drop down the long scree slope below Bristly Ridge to the pass, Bwlch Tryfan. Cross the wall by one of the stiles and follow the Miners' Track (see p.56) back to the car park.

* The Reserve was established in 1954 and is owned by the National Trust. Its popularity is attributable to it being a mountain reserve within easy reach of a main road. The rock basin, the nucleus of the reserve, was carved out during the Pleistocene Ice Age by intense glacial erosion. Twll Du, the dark cleft in the basin headwall and Llyn Idwal, famed in legend and retained by morainic debris, can be seen from the reserve entrance.

ROUTE 15

Discloses the remarkable effects on the landscape of the most recent glaciation, the late Devensian, which ended in Britain just 11 000 years ago. For experienced walkers.

Group	Glyder
Number of summits	4
Time required	4¾ hours
Map	O.S. 1:25 000 Outdoor Leisure Sheet 17
Start	At 649603 — Ogwen car park
Parking	Car park at the start (further facilities east along the A5)
Nearest centre	Bethesda (7km)

1st Summit 10 Y GARN
947m   630595
Carries a stone shelter.

2nd Summit 27 FOEL GOCH
831m   628612
The watchtower of Nant Ffrancon. Marked by a cairn.

3rd Summit 31 MYNYDD PERFEDD
812m   623618
Marked by a cairn.

4th Summit 30 CARNEDD Y FILIAST
822m   620627
Carries a stone shelter.

Go to the rear of the car park toilet block and cross the stile in the gorge (known for unfortunate reasons as 'Tin Can Alley'). At the end of the gorge, ascend right, cross the stile and turn left onto the path. Cross the stile in the fence, step over the low wall and pass through the gap in the higher wall. Then mount the sharply rising path and make headway up the ridge crest where, slowly, the intriguing hanging valley, Cwm Clyd, comes into view. Keep to the path and in time, on attaining a small stony plateau (in mist sometimes mistaken for Y Garn summit), continue forward and ascend a further 200m to the summit. Go back to the plateau, descend north-west and follow the path to the head of Cwm Cywion. Then bear right off the path and follow the fence to the second summit, Foel Goch. Cross the stile, drop down to the path deserted earlier and turn right. Continue downslope to the pass, Bwlch y Brecan, keep right at the fork and make the stiff pull to Mynydd Perfedd, the third summit. Now head due north and approaching the head of the glacial hollow, Cwm Graianog, which overlooks the vast U-shaped Nant Ffrancon Valley, bear left to the wall and cross the stile to the fourth and final summit, Carnedd y Filiast.

To return, head north-east and drop down the steep scree-covered mountainside where there are traces of a path. Where the slope gradient eases, resist the temptation to stray to the left, keep north-east and negotiate more steep ground. Aim for the sharp bend in the old valley road, pass Tai Newyddion (a naval mountain training base) and follow the road back past Idwal Cottage* to the car park.

* Idwal Cottage, now a youth hostel, was built originally as a hunting lodge. It was once the home of a quarrymaster and later an annexe to Ogwen Cottage.** Opening in 1931, the hostel was one of the first in Britain. It was extended in 1962 as a memorial to Alf Embleton.*** The extension was officially opened in May 1963 by Colonel Gerald Haythornthwaite, President of the Ramblers' Association, who presented the key to Mr R. Emrys Jones, Chairman of Merseyside YHA. Mrs Embleton unveiled a tablet inside the extension. The extension was paid for by the Embleton commemorative fund organised by the Ramblers' Association. The fund also financed the construction of the stile where the path leaves the A5 at the foot of Pen yr Ole Wen.

** Ogwen Cottage, an old coaching inn, has been associated with walkers for more than a century. In 1965, it was bought by the City of Birmingham Council for use as an outdoor pursuit centre. It was modernised in 1967 and extended in 1976.

*** Alfred Embleton was born on Merseyside in 1898. In 1922, he helped create the Liverpool Federation of Rambling Clubs. In

1929, he was one of those who founded the Youth Hostel movement in Merseyside (an area later responsible for the running of two chains of hostels in North Wales). In 1930, with Arthur Roberts of the Ramblers' Association, he visited Austria and Germany to find out about the work of the movements there. (The world's first youth hostel was opened in 1910 by the German schoolmaster, Richard Schirrmann.) In 1935, Embleton was appointed the first treasurer of the Ramblers' Association, a post he held until he died in April 1961. Roberts, a Chairman of the English Council of the Association, played a leading role in the decision to commemorate Alf, aware of his lifetime's contribution to ramblers and youth hostels throughout Britain.

ROUTE 16

Finds seclusion in an otherwise popular area. A demanding walk; do not attempt unless in good shape.

Group	Glyder
Number of summits	1
Time required	3½ hours
Map	O.S. 1:25 000 Outdoor Leisure Sheet 17
Start	At 607582 — Nant Peris car park
Parking	Car park at the start
Nearest centre	Llanberis (4km)

The Summit 13 ELIDIR FAWR
924m   **611613**
Carries a stone shelter. The peak's broad south shoulder remains disfigured by the terraces of the once thriving Dinorwig Quarry.* The existence of Dinorwig Power Station,** however, is less evident.

From the car park entrance, turn left to Rehoboth Chapel, turn right and follow the lane. At the end of the lane, pass through the gate onto the path, go over the stile crossing the wall and progress to the river, the Afon Dudodyn. Cross the single handrail bridge and head due north up the laborious mountainside where there are traces of a path. Go over the stile crossing the wall, press on upslope and slowly move right to the boulder field. Then gradually ascend beneath the summit ridge to gain it, hopefully, as near to the shelter as possible.

Return by the same route.

* Dinorwig Quarry, once the second largest slate quarry in the world, was first worked on a small scale in the 1770s. The first serious exploitation of slate from Dinorwig was by the landowner Thomas Assheton Smith in 1809. In December 1842, the quarry was linked by the Padarn Rail Road direct to Port Dinorwig from where the slate was shipped to all corners of the earth. Employing over 3000 men, its peak of production was reached in

the late 1890s, but slowly, as the use of artificial substitutes and competition from foreign markets increased, the work-force was reduced, dropping eventually to 300. The quarry closed in 1969.

** Dinorwig Power Station, the largest hydro-electric pumped storage power station in Europe, commenced operations in December 1981. It was officially opened in May 1984 by the Prince of Wales. Built for the CEGB at a cost of over £400 million, the station can supply 1320 megawatts to the national grid in under ten seconds.

ROUTE 17

A superior circuit incorporating the magnificent but menacing rock peak of Tryfan. To be attempted only by experienced walkers familiar with rock scrambling.

Group	Glyder
Number of summits	3
Time required	4¼ hours
Map	O.S. 1:25 000 Outdoor Leisure Sheet 17
Start	At 663602 — Milestone layby
Parking	Layby at the start (further facilities west along the A5)
Nearest centre	Bethesda (8km)

1st Summit **15 TRYFAN**
915m 663593
One of the most challenging and entertaining mountains in Britain where John Hunt (see p.88) and Edmund Hillary trained for the historic 1953 Everest expedition. Adam and Eve, the celebrated monoliths crowning the summit, are often mistaken for two climbers while travelling west along the A5 from Capel Curig.

2nd Summit **35 Y FOEL GOCH**
805m 677582
Also known as the Nameless Peak. The summit is marked by a cairn.

3rd Summit **47 GALLT YR OGOF**
763m 685585
Marked by a cairn.

Cross the layby stile, follow the rocky stairway and ascend beside the wall towards the popular rhyolite climbing crag, the Milestone Buttress (named after the milestone that once stood near the layby). Bear left across the boulder slope and ascend below Tryfan's classic north ridge. On gaining the shoulder, where the landscape to the east is revealed, mount the spiralling scree path which soon becomes absorbed into the ridge's labyrinth of boot-smoothed trails and paths. From hereon, it is difficult to define a precise passage up the ridge but try to keep to its centre, where the paths are less exposed and eroded and the scrambling sections more accommodating. In any event, all the paths and numerous trails of worn rock lead to the castellated summit area. From here, head south-west and drop down across the boulder-covered flank of the south ridge to the pass, Bwlch Tryfan. Turn left onto the Miners' Track,* cross the wall by one of the stiles and follow the track to the head of Cwm Tryfan. Then take the path leading east and pass the tarn, Llyn y Gaseg Fraith (one of the highest in Wales). Ascend to the second summit, Y Foel Goch, continue along the path and just past the pool, where the path bends right, bear left to Gallt yr Ogof, the third and final summit.

To return, descend north-west into Cwm Gwern Gof and cross the stream draining it, the Nant yr Ogof. Drop down further in line with the stream, go over the stile crossing the fence and pass the farmhouse, Gwern Gof Isaf. Turn left onto the A5 and walk back to the layby.

* The Miners' Track, an ancient pathway, was consolidated in the early nineteenth century. It was used by miners living in Bethesda as the link between their homes — a weekend comfort only — and the Brittania Copper Mine, a daunting return journey of over 35km. During the week the men lodged in damp windswept barracks, the remains of which still exist (see p.42).

ROUTE 18

Offers gratifying views for comparatively little effort. Suitable for casual walkers and family groups.

Group	Glyder
Number of summits	1
Time required	1½ hours
Map	O.S. 1:25 000 Outdoor Leisure Sheet 17
Start	At 579657 — Rhiwlas Post Office
Parking	Limited roadside in the village
Nearest centre	Bethesda (8km)

The Summit 197 MOELYCI
      410m   **593659**
      Marked by a cairn.

From the post office, follow the ascending lane (Wesley Street) and at the junction near the church, continue forward. After 600m, just past the entrance to Cae'r Gof Farm, turn right onto the narrow path, bear right onto the track and pass through the gate. At the junction, where there are two gates, pass through the gate ahead, make a U-turn and pass through the wall gap. Turn right onto the heather slope, pass the lone boulder and cross the sizeable summit plateau to the cairn.

Return by the same route.

ROUTE 19

A summiteer's seventh heaven. A sporting but toilsome exploit.
For experienced walkers.

Group	Carneddau
Number of summits	7
Time required	7 hours
Map	O.S. 1:25 000 Outdoor Leisure Sheet 17
Start	At 623668 — Bethesda car park
Parking	Car park at the start
Nearest centre	Bethesda

1st Summit 9 YR ELEN
962m   673651
Marked by a cairn.

2nd Summit 3 CARNEDD LLYWELYN
1064m   683643
Probably named after the only native Prince of
Wales, Llywelyn ap Gruffudd (Llywelyn the
Last).* A theological group in Los Angeles
recognises Carnedd Llywelyn as one of the holy
mountains of the world. The vast summit area
carries the remains of an ancient burial cairn.

3rd Summit 8 FOEL GRACH
976m   688658
Carries an ancient burial cairn and a refuge hut.
The hut was built in 1964 for the sole purpose of
providing shelter in emergencies.

4th Summit 12 GARNEDD UCHAF
926m   687669
A wild boulder-strewn summit at the heart of the
group. Marked by a cairn.

5th Summit 34 BERA BACH
807m   672677
Unmarked.

6th Summit   40 BERA MAWR
794m   674682
Unmarked.

7th Summit   49 DROSGL
758m   663680
Carries the remains of two Bronze Age burial
cairns, excavated in 1976. The larger cairn covered
two cists which had been robbed, probably in the
late nineteenth century. However, deposits of
cremated bone and a whetstone were retrieved
from under the cist slabs. The smaller cairn
concealed one cist which entombed an un-
disturbed cremation deposit, possibly of a young
adult female.

From the car park, go to the High Street, turn left and turn left
again onto Pen y Bryn Road. Bear right onto Pantglas Road,
eventually pass Gerlan Post Office and just past the second
bridge which spans the Afon Llafar, keep left to the entrance to
Bangor Waterworks. Cross the stile, continue forward and cross
the next stile. Turn right to the wall gap, go to the rear of the
derelict homestead and mount the path beside the wall. Cross
the stream, the Afon Cenllusg, cross the stile and follow the path
beside the Llafar. Pass through the gaps and in time, where the
path begins to descend, cross the river, aim north of east across
the moor and climb sharply to the ridge step. Then make
the steep pull to the first summit, Yr Elen. Head south-east and
follow the path to Carnedd Llywelyn, the second summit. Drop
down just east of north and pick up the firmly established ridge
path which crosses the third summit, Foel Grach. Approaching
the fourth summit and pursuing the lower ground, the path
bends right. At this point, ascend to the summit, Garnedd
Uchaf, head north-west and drop down through the heather,
past the craggy bluffs of Yr Aryg to the castellated summit of
Bera Bach. Proceed north-east the short distance to the
penultimate summit, Bera Mawr. Then head south-west through
more heather to the seventh and final summit, Drosgl.

To return, descend due south to the track (a former packhorse
trail), turn right and after 400m, where the track veers right, bear

left to the humps of the spur, Gyrn Wigau. Drop down to the wall junction, pass through the gate and follow the track. After about 800m, turn left onto the graded track and at the T-junction, turn right to the car park.

* Llywelyn ap Gruffudd was born about 1230. He was a descendant of Gruffudd ap Cynan, one of Gwynedd's most remarkable rulers. In 1267, in the Treaty of Montgomery, Llywelyn was formally recognised by Henry III as the Prince of all Wales. Ten years later, however, during the early reign of the succeeding King, Edward I, one of the most resolute monarchs that England ever produced, Llywelyn was shorn of power outside Gwynedd in the Treaty of Aberconwy. In October 1278, he married Eleanor de Montfort, daughter of Edward's old enemy, Simon. In June 1282, Eleanor died giving birth to a daughter, Gwenllian. Six months later, at Cilmeri near Builth Wells, Llywelyn was slain in battle by the English lancer, Stephen de Frankton, who was unaware of whom he had killed. (Gwenllian was their only child and was cared for and raised in a Lincolnshire nunnery where she spent the rest of her life. She died in February 1337.) On recognising the dead Prince, who was found to be unarmed, the lancer severed his head. It was washed in a stream, sent to Edward at Rhuddlan and later exhibited on the Tower of London's highest pinnacle. The Prince's decapitated body is interred, it is thought, in the grounds of Abbey Cwm-hir, the once famous Cistercian establishment near Rhayader, founded in 1176 by Cadwallon ap Madog, Lord of Maelienydd and cousin of Deheubarth's greatest ruler, the Lord Rhys. In 1902, a small monument was erected on the spot at Cilmeri where Llywelyn is believed to have been killed. This was replaced in 1956 by a large obelisk of Trefor Grey Granite (see p.26) from his native Gwynedd. In the courtyard of the Gwynedd County Headquarters at Caernarfon, a slate plinth commemorates the seventh centenary of the Prince's death, a reminder of his last gallant stand for the liberties of his beloved country. The plinth was unveiled in December 1982 by Councillor W.R.P. George, Chairman of the County Council and nephew of the former Prime Minister, David Lloyd George.

ROUTE 20

Confronts the south corner bastion of the great Carneddau Ridge and probably demands the most strenuous walking in Wales.

Group	Carneddau
Number of summits	2
Time required	4½ hours
Map	O.S. 1:25 000 Outdoor Leisure Sheet 17
Start	At 649603 — Ogwen car park
Parking	Car park at the start (further facilities east along the A5)
Nearest centre	Bethesda (7km)

1st Summit 7 PEN YR OLE WEN
978m   **655619**
Marked by a cairn.

2nd Summit 4 CARNEDD DAFYDD
1044m   **662630**
Probably named after Dafydd ap Gruffudd,* younger brother of Llywelyn the Last and grandson of Llywelyn ab Iorwerth (Llywelyn the Great). The summit carries an ancient burial cairn mutilated by the incorporation of shelters.

From the car park, turn left onto the A5 and just past the bridge, cross the Alf Embleton memorial stile (see p.51). Turn left onto the path, pass the holly tree and climb sharply to a small grassy platform from where a number of faint paths set out. Mount the cairned path, ascend through the heather and bear left of the rock wall onto the bare scree slope. At the fork above the wall, bear right, persevere upslope and resist any temptation to stray from the main ascending path, especially to the east. The path eventually passes a conspicuous cairn near a stone shelter, levels out across the ridge crest and leads to the Pen yr Ole Wen summit cairn (about the same altitude as England's highest). From here, head north-west and pick up the path circling the head of Cwm Lloer. The path cuts through the tumbled remains of the ancient cairn, Carnedd Fach, passes a similar ruined cairn and rises to the second summit, Carnedd Dafydd.

To return, go back to the Pen yr Ole Wen summit cairn, head east and drop down the shattered ridge crest where there are traces of a path. At the foot of the ridge, near the tarn, Ffynnon Lloer, cross the plateau to the stream draining the tarn, the Afon Lloer, continue downslope and go over the stile crossing the wall. After about 500m, cross the stream towards the farmhouse, Tal y Llyn Ogwen, cross the Holywell High School stile** and turn right beneath the power lines. Bear left onto the farm track, pass Glan Dena (a mountaineering club base) and follow the A5 back to the car park.

* Dafydd ap Gruffudd, who once marched with the English, assumed national leadership in December 1282 following the death of Llywelyn (see p.60). In March of that year, the Second War of Welsh Independence, the turmoil during which Llywelyn was slaughtered, was started by the unpredictable Dafydd. He had launched a night-time attack on the English-occupied Hawarden Castle. Now though, with the irreplaceable Llywelyn gone — a morale-deflating blow for the Welsh Army — the war was as good as lost. For a while, Dafydd held off the advancing Edwardian forces but in January 1283, the Conwy was crossed and Dolwyddelan taken. His last stronghold, Castell y Bere in Meirionnydd, fell in April and two months later, betrayed by his own people, he was captured. His execution, in Shrewsbury in October, was the first in Britain for reasons of rebellion for two hundred years.

** The stile, a sturdy ladder type, was positioned in 1970. Made from elm purchased from a Holywell sawmill, it was constructed by the school's woodwork and metalwork departments during lunch hours and after school. The school's County Council own an outdoor pursuits centre at Nant Bwlch-yr-haearn, near Betws-y-coed.

ROUTE 21

For the mountain connoisseur. An arduous excursion.

Group	Carneddau
Number of summits	4
Time required	5¼ hours
Map	O.S. 1:25 000 Outdoor Leisure Sheet 16
Start	At 743693 — the road-track junction near Bwlch y Gaer Farm
Parking	Parking area at the junction
Nearest centre	Llanrwst (12km)

1st Summit   130 PEN Y CASTELL
623m   **721688**
The highest point is unmarked.

2nd Summit   44 DRUM
770m   **708695**
Carries an ancient burial cairn mutilated and extensively remodelled to form a spacious shelter.

3rd Summit   11 FOEL FRAS
942m   **696681**
Carries a trig pillar.

4th Summit   25 LLWYTMOR
849m   **689692**
Carries several rudimentary cairns, any of which could surmount the highest point.

From the parking area, head south-west along the higher of the two tracks (a former packhorse trail), bear right at the fork and pass through the gates. In the shadow of the unmistakable crag, Craig Cefn Coch, pass through the fence gate, bear left and ascend to the first summit, Pen y Castell. Drop down north-west, cross the stile at the junction and continue forward. Follow the fence up the long broken ridge flank to Drum, the second summit, continue beside the fence leading south and pass the enclosure. Then make the tiresome ascent to Foel Fras, the third summit. Descend north-west, cross the saddle and head upslope to Llwytmor, the fourth and final summit.

To return, go back towards Foel Fras, cross its broad north shoulder back to the fence and turn left. Pass the enclosure, cross the stile in the fence and drop down due east to the fence junction. Bear right onto the path, descend to the gate and walk back to the parking area.

ROUTE 22

A hard trek on shelterless hills.

Group	Carneddau
Number of summits	2
Time required	4½ hours
Map	O.S. 1:25 000 Outdoor Leisure Sheet 16
Start	At 720581 — Capel Curig Post Office
Parking	Limited roadside in the village
Nearest centre	Betws-y-coed (8km)

1st Summit **38 PENLLITHRIG-Y-WRACH**
799m   **716623**
Carries a low pile of stones, possibly the remains of
an ancient burial cairn.

2nd Summit **26 PEN YR HELGI DU**
833m   **697630**
Marked by a cairn.

From the post office, head north along the A5 and after about
900m, near the power lines, pass through the gate and follow the
path. Pass the farmhouse, Tal y Waun, go over the stile crossing
the wall and follow the path across the moor. Cross the bridge
spanning the leat, turn left beside the fence and pass through the
gate. Cross the bridge, continue forward 100m and bear right
across the rough grassland. Then climb the laborious hillside to
the first summit, Penllithrig-y-wrach. Drop down north-west to
the pass, Bwlch y Tri Marchog, cross the stile onto the path and
progress upslope to Pen yr Helgi Du, the second summit.

To return, head south and drop down the crest of the long gentle
ridge. Pass through the wall gap, bear left at the fork and go over
the stile crossing the fence. Cross the bridge spanning the leat,
drop down to the wall gate and turn right onto the farm track.
Pass Tal y Braich Isaf Farmhouse to the A5, turn left and walk
back to Capel Curig.

ROUTE 23

Penetrates a bleak yet captivating land. For experienced walkers.

Group	Carneddau
Number of summits	4
Time required	5 hours
Map	O.S. 1:25 000 Outdoor Leisure Sheet 16
Start	At 720581 — Capel Curig Post Office
Parking	Limited roadside in the village
Nearest centre	Betws-y-coed (8km)

1st Summit   **185 CRIMPIAU**
               475m   **733595**
               The summit is marked by a cairn.

2nd Summit   **171 CRAIG WEN**
               548m   **729602**
               A surprising viewpoint. Marked by a cairn.

3rd Summit   **85 CREIGIAU GLEISION**
               678m   **728615**
               Marked by a cairn.

4th Summit   **116 PEN COWLYD**
               634m   **733622**
               Not named on the map. Marked by a cairn.

Opposite the post office, go over the stile next to the gate, follow the path and pass beneath the power lines. Pass through the wall gap, bear right at the fork and go over the stile to enter the wood. Follow the path through the wood, pass through the gate and go over the bridge spanning the stream, the Nant y Geuallt. Bear left at the fork, continue beside the fence and follow the stream into the rising valley. In due course, cross the stream to head due west and ascend to Crimpiau, the first summit. Drop down north-west to the wall, continue forward and pass through the gaps. Then make the sharp pull to the second summit, Craig Wen. From here, head due north, pick up the faint and intermittent path and ascend along the undulating ridge crest to

Creigiau Gleision, the third summit. The path, now more distinct, leads north-east to the fourth and final summit, Pen Cowlyd.

To return, continue north-east to the fence-line and drop down to Cowlyd Reservoir.* Cross the dam, turn left and follow the path. Cross the inflow by the bridge, pass through the gate and make headway beside the fence. Cross the bridge spanning the leat, follow the path across the moor and go over the stile crossing the wall. Pass the farmhouse, Tal y Waun, pass through the gate onto the A5 and walk back to Capel Curig.

* Cowlyd Reservoir, originally a natural lake, was converted between 1901 and 1904 to supply water to the Conwy and Colwyn Bay areas. Situated in a bleak steep-sided valley, the reservoir is the deepest in North Wales with a maximum depth of 68m. In 1915, a year of an unusually long summer drought, the area's Water Supply Board sought an increase in Cowlyd's capacity. The following year, permission was granted to construct a new dam, 13m higher than the existing one, together with a tramway for maintenance purposes. The work was completed in December 1921 and the official opening took place in September 1922. On New Year's Eve 1924, however, a section of the dam gave way and two years further work was necessary. By 1967, the reservoir could be reached by a motorable track, allowing maintenance vehicles direct access. The tramway was closed as a result.

ROUTE 24

Collars the two northernmost 600m summits in Wales with relative ease. Suitable for novice walkers.

Group	Carneddau
Number of summits	2
Time required	1¾ hours
Map	O.S. 1:25 000 Outdoor Leisure Sheet 16
Start	At 731714 — the road-track junction near Cae Coch cottage
Parking	Limited roadside at the junction
Nearest centre	Conwy (10km)

1st Summit 142 TAL Y FAN
 610m   729726
 Carries a trig pillar.

2nd Summit 150 FOEL LWYD
 603m   720723
 Marked by a cairn.

From the junction, take the road leading west (an old Roman road laid down about AD 100), go over the stile crossing the wall and follow the path. Cross two more stiles, turn left and pass the next stile. Then ascend beside the wall to Tal y Fan, the first summit. Go back and cross the stile passed previously and follow the wall leading west. On reaching Foel Lwyd, the second summit, pass through the gap to emerge by the cairn.

To return, head south-east to the wall and drop down the long gentle slope beside it. Pass through the gate, turn left onto the Roman road and walk back to the junction.

ROUTE 25

Probes deceptively inviting country. In mist, the proficient use of map and compass will be essential.

Group	Carneddau
Number of summits	3
Time required	2¾ hours
Map	O.S. 1:25 000 Outdoor Leisure Sheet 17
Start	At 630671 — Tan y Foel cottages, Cilfodan, Bethesda
Parking	Limited roadside at the start
Nearest centre	Bethesda

1st Summit **198 MOEL FABAN**
409m 634679
Carries three ancient burial cairns. In the mid-nineteenth century, a cist containing a Bronze Age urn was found beneath the largest cairn.

2nd Summit **172 Y GURN**
542m 647687
Marked by a cairn.

3rd Summit **160 MOEL WNION**
580m 649697
Carries an ancient burial cairn surmounted by a trig pillar.

From the cottages, head north along the track, pass through the gates and continue forward to Moel Faban, the first summit. Drop down north-east, pick up the distant path and at the fork, bear left. Cross the traversing track, pass the quarry remains and ascend sharply across the rocks to Y Gurn, the second summit. Then drop down north where the rocks give way to grass, cross the rutted track (a former packhorse trail) and climb the hillside to Moel Wnion, the third and final summit.

To return, head due west, drop down to the junction and turn left onto the descending path (another old packhorse route). After about 250m, keep left at the fork, cross the streams and pass the sheepfold. At the next fork, keep right and continue beside the wall. Where the wall turns right, bear left at the fork, pass through the gate and walk back to the cottages.

ROUTE 26

A quiet stroll along an easily followed track. Ideal for introducing younger children to hill walking.

Group	Carneddau
Number of summits	1
Time required	1½ hours
Map	O.S. 1:50 000 Landranger Sheet 115
Start	At 699747 — the end of Mount Road, Llanfairfechan
Parking	Limited roadside at the start
Nearest centre	Llanfairfechan

The Summit 193 MOELFRE
         435m   717744

Old legends have it that three women were turned into stone on the hilltop. The women lived on the coastal plain to the north of the hill where their job was to winnow the corn that had been harvested (a chore where corn is thrown into a breeze to separate the chaff from the grain). At this particular time, there had been no wind for many days so the women, tired of waiting, humped the corn in sacks to the top of Moelfre where a breeze was assured. However, as the women had been warned, the day was the Sabbath. For a while, the breeze was gentle and all was well but suddenly, the gusts grew stronger, the skies darkened menacingly and in no time at all, the women were transformed into stone. In January 1944, disaster struck here again — a Consolidated B-24 Liberator bomber from RAF Valley crashed into the foot of the hill, killing six of the crew of eleven. The summit of the hill is unmarked.

At the end of the road, pass through the gate and follow the farm track. Pass through the gates at Blaen Llwyn Farm (not named on the map), continue along the track and pass through more gates. Keep left at the fork, ascend to the wall and turn right to the summit.

Return by the same route.

ROUTE 27

Along one of the best stretches of Offa's Dyke Path.* An excellent family walk.

Group	Clwydian
Number of summits	2
Time required	2¼ hours
Map	O.S. 1:50 000 Landranger Sheet 116
Start	At 161605 — Bwlch Pen Barras car parks
Parking	Car parks at the start
Nearest centre	Ruthin (5km)

1st Summit **168 MOEL FAMA**
555m **161626**
Crowned by the restored remains of the Jubilee Tower.**

2nd Summit **186 MOEL DYWYLL**
475m **151632**
Carries two cairns, the less conspicuous marks the highest point.

From the north-west car park, follow Offa's Dyke Path, ignoring the track beside the fence, keep left at the fork and continue to the first summit, Moel Fama. Then head north-west and follow the Path beside the wall to Moel Dywyll, the second summit.

To return, go back along the Path for about 700m where it begins to steepen, bear right onto the narrow ascending path and cross the gentle heather slope. Rejoin the Dyke Path, turn right and walk back to the car parks.

* Offa's Dyke Path, the fourth long-distance footpath to be designated as such in Britain, runs from Prestatyn in the north to Sedbury in the south, a distance of about 270km. It was officially opened in July 1971 by Lord Hunt of Everest. It is named after the longest earthwork in Britain, Offa's Dyke, which was constructed in the late eighth century. The Dyke was built by Offa as a barrier between his midland kingdom of Mercia and his turbulent Welsh neighbours. Both the Path and the Dyke closely follow the present-day border between England and Wales. Offa was the most illustrious of all Anglo-Saxon rulers, born about 735. After a short civil war in 757, he emerged as King of Mercia and overlord of all England south of the Humber. He died near Rhuddlan in 796 while attempting to complete the final stretch of the Dyke to the sea. His burial place, by the Ouse at Bedford, has long since been washed away by the river.

** The Jubilee Tower was built in 1810 to commemorate the Golden Jubilee of George III. It was designed by the Chester architect, Thomas Harrison. In 1862, the tower collapsed during a storm and for more than a century it lay in ruins. In 1970, European Conservation Year, its base was rebuilt by volunteers and the steel view pointers were installed.

ROUTE 28

Visits an ancient British settlement. A short sharp ascent.

Group	Clwydian
Number of summits	1
Time required	¾ hour
Map	O.S. 1:50 000 Landranger Sheet 116
Start	At 161605 — Bwlch Pen Barras car parks
Parking	Car parks at the start
Nearest centre	Ruthin (5km)

The Summit 177 FOEL FENLLI
511m   164600

Crowned by the highest known Iron Age settlement in Wales. It is the most southerly of Clwyd's unique chain of hilltop settlements which may have been founded by the Deceangli tribe shortly before the Roman invasion of Celtic Britain.* In July 1816, over 1500 Roman coins were found on the hilltop, some of which are now in the Grosvenor Museum, Chester.

To the rear of the south side car park, pass through the gate, turn right and pass through the fence gate. Bear left onto the path (a relocation of Offa's Dyke Path) which higher up moves back to the fence, pass the stile and continue upslope. Turn left at the T-junction and after a few metres, bear right at the fork to the summit cairn.

Return by the same route.

* The Roman conquest of Britain began in AD 43 during the reign of the Emperor Claudius, almost a hundred years after the two fact-finding expeditions by Julius Caesar. The main assault force landed in Kent, under the command of Aulus Plautius. It consisted of four legions: the II Augusta from Strasbourg; the XIV Gemina from Mainz; the XX Valeria from Neuss; and the IX Hispana from Pannonia. The conquest of Wales was finally achieved, after a bitter struggle, in AD 78 when the thirty-nine-year-old Julius Agricola defeated the tough Ordovices tribe.

ROUTE 29

A short tour of fascinating territory. Ideal for introducing younger children to hill walking.

Group	Clwydian
Number of summits	2
Time required	1 hour
Map	O.S. 1:50 000 Landranger Sheet 116
Start	At 146657 — the junction of the Groes Fawr-Star Crossing road and Offa's Dyke Path (Star Crossing — not named on the map)
Parking	Parking area at the junction
Nearest centre	Denbigh (10km)

1st Summit   **188 MOEL ARTHUR**
                         455m   **145660**

Crowned by an ancient British settlement, said to be, among others, the burial place of Boudicca.* In 1849, shallow excavations on the hilltop unearthed pieces of Roman pottery and fragments of flint arrowheads.

2nd Summit   **196 MOEL PLAS-YW**
                         419m   **152668**

Marked by a cairn.

From the parking area, pass through the gate, bear right and follow the path (a relocation of Offa's Dyke Path). After about 250m, turn left onto the steep path and ascend direct to the Moel Arthur summit cairn. Head north-east, drop down along the track and pass through the fence gate. Continue forward, cross the traversing track and ascend to Moel Plas-yw, the second summit.

To return, go back to the traversing track, turn left and pass through the gates. Turn right onto the road and walk back to the parking area.

* Boudicca (sometimes spelt Boadicea), 'Queen of the Britons', was the wife of Prasutagus, King of the Iceni tribe. The King's

75

death in AD 60, during the early Principate, sparked off one of the most determined revolts against Roman rule in any province. Having made the Emperor Nero co-heir in his will, Prasutagus had presumably envisaged the appointment of his wife as his successor. However, Roman officials, remembering that Cartimandua (Queen of the Brigantes tribe) was an encumbrance rather than an asset, ignored Boudicca's claim to rulership and absorbed the Norfolk kingdom into the province. Boudicca's protests caused her to be flogged and her daughters raped. This humiliation drove her Icenian warriors, backed by their Trinovantian neighbours — long incensed by Roman brutality — into open rebellion. About 2000 men of Legio IX Hispana and 500 auxiliaries, under the command of Petilius Cerialis who escaped to Lincoln, were massacred at Colchester. London, next to feel the wrath of the Boudiccan onslaught, perished amid slaughter and Verulamium (near St Albans) encountered the same fate. The greatest loss of life, however, reported to have been near Fenny Stratford (Bucks), came when the revolt was crushed by the elite Legio XIV Gemina, led by Suetonius Paulinus. Boudicca is thought to have poisoned herself and her final resting place is more likely to be in England than in Wales, probably near Northampton.

ROUTE 30

Follows Offa's Dyke Path to the most extensive of the ancient Clwydian settlements. Suitable for any able-bodied person.

Group	Clwydian
Number of summits	1
Time required	1 hour
Map	O.S. 1:50 000 Landranger Sheet 116
Start	At 139668 — the junction of the Llangwyfan-Nannerch road and Offa's Dyke Path
Parking	Parking area at the junction
Nearest centre	Denbigh (9km)

The Summit 192 PEN Y CLODDIAU
439m   **127678**

One of the largest known prehistoric fortified settlements in Wales. The inner rampart encloses an oval shaped stronghold of about 20ha. There are traces of hut circles in the north-east corner.

From the parking area, pass through the gate to enter the forest, mount Offa's Dyke Path and progress in line with the gently rising perimeter fence. Cross the stile and shortly, where the Path and fence turn left, continue forward, follow the track and proceed to the summit cairn.

Return by the same route.

ROUTE 31
Provides unrivalled panoramic views. An energetic walk.

Group	Moelwyni
Number of summits	1
Time required	3 hours
Map	O.S. 1:25 000 Outdoor Leisure Sheet 16
Start	At 711577 — the layby on the south side of the A4086
Parking	Layby at the start
Nearest centre	Betws-y-coed (9km)

The Summit 22 MOEL SIABOD
872m   **705546**
Carries a trig pillar, a stone shelter and the remains of an ancient burial cairn. The cairn has been robbed of material for the construction of the shelter.

From the layby, follow the road east to Plas y Brenin,* pass through the gate and drop down to the outflow of Llynnau Mymbyr. Go over the bridge, cross the track and take the rising path into Coed Bryn Engan (part of the 8100ha Gwydir Forest which includes 2800ha of grazing and farming land). Turn right at the T-junction and at the access road, turn left. After 10m, turn right, continue along the path and just past the second stile, bear right to the open mountainside. Then follow the path to the summit.

Return by the same route.

* Plas y Brenin is the National Mountaineering Centre for England and Wales, administered by the Sports Council. It was first used as an outdoor pursuit centre known as The Snowdonia National Recreation Centre in 1955. The original building, a small coaching house, the Capel Curig Inn, was built about 1800 by Richard Pennant (slate magnate, made Baron Penrhyn in 1783). Serving dried goat as its speciality, the inn soon flourished and for several years was a staging post for the Royal Mail

coaches which carried the Irish Mail between Shrewsbury and Holyhead. By 1860, having attracted such eminent guests as Sir Walter Scott and Sir Joseph Paxton, the inn had prospered into a fifty-roomed hotel. It was renamed the Royal Hotel in 1870 after a visit by Queen Victoria. During the Second World War, the hotel was used as a mountain warfare training centre. It reopened as a hotel in 1946 until 1953. Details of courses at Plas y Brenin can be obtained by writing to: The National Centre for Mountain Activities, Plas y Brenin, Capel Curig, Gwynedd, LL24 0ET.

ROUTE 32

A premier mountain excursion. For experienced walkers.

Group	Moelwyni
Number of summits	2
Time required	3½ hours
Map	O.S. 1:25 000 Outdoor Leisure Sheet 18
Start	At 631446 — Croesor car park
Parking	Car park at the start
Nearest centre	Porthmadog (11km)

1st Summit **45 MOELWYN MAWR**
770m   **658448**
One of the great summit viewpoints of Wales.
Carries a trig pillar.

2nd Summit **70 MOELWYN BACH**
710m   **660437**
Marked by a cairn.

From the car park entrance, turn left and at the crossroads, continue forward. Pass through the gate, turn left and ascend roughly in line with the wall where there are traces of a path. Go over the stile crossing the wall, make headway onto the ridge and gradually move left to the fence. Where the fence turns left, cross the stile, follow the wall and pass the stone tower (once associated with Fron Boeth Slate Quarry which closed in 1914). Then ascend along the narrowing ridge crest to the first summit, Moelwyn Mawr. Descend south-east, follow the path between the craggy bluffs and climb to the crest of the rocky elevation, Craig Ysgafn, high above Stwlan Reservoir.* Now drop down sharply to that most perfect of cols, Bwlch Stwlan. Ignore the path ahead, bear right onto the grassy path and ascend to Moelwyn Bach, the second summit.

To return, head west, drop down the crest of the long gentle ridge and cross the stile. Pass through the gates, turn right onto the road and walk back to Croesor.

* Stwlan Reservoir, originally a small corrie lake, was converted in the late 1950s to store water for Ffestiniog Power Station. The reservoir's huge concrete dam, a popular viewpoint, is accessible by road from the Power Station Information Centre at Tanygrisiau. The power station can supply 360 megawatts to the national grid in under one minute. It was the CEGB's first hydro-electric pumped storage power station to be built in Wales, commencing operations in December 1961. It was officially opened in August 1963 by the Queen.

ROUTE 33

North Wales at its most rugged. A severe walk; do not attempt unless in good shape.

Group	Moelwyni
Number of summits	6
Time required	8¼ hours
Map	O.S. 1:25 000 Outdoor Leisure Sheet 17
Start	At 627506 — Pont Bethania car park
Parking	Car park at the start
Nearest centre	Beddgelert (5km)

1st Summit   **80 CNICHT**
                 689m   **645466**
                 Often referred to as 'the Welsh Matterhorn', a tribute also associated with Cribyn in the Brecon Beacons. The summit is marked by a cairn.

2nd Summit   **110 MOEL YR HYDD**
                 648m   **672454**
                 Unmarked.

3rd Summit   **74 ALLT FAWR**
                 698m   **681474**
                 Marked by a cairn.

4th Summit   **87 MOEL DRUMAN**
                 676m   **671476**
                 Unmarked.

5th Summit   **90 YSGAFELL WEN (SOUTH)**
                 672m   **666481**
                 Marked by a cairn.

6th Summit   **93 YSGAFELL WEN (NORTH)**
                 669m   **663485**
                 Marked by a cairn.

From the car park, follow the road south for 400m, turn left onto the lane and go over the bridge spanning the river, the Afon

Glaslyn. Pass through the gates, turn right with the lane and after about 1km, cross the bridge to the rear of Gelli Iago (once a farmhouse now an outdoor pursuits centre). Cross the bridge onto the path, climb sharply to the wall gap and progress to the shallow pass, Bwlch y Batel. Go over the stile crossing the wall, bear left to the wall gap and follow the path. In due course, mount the scree-covered gully, turn left onto Cnicht's south-west ridge path and circumvent the rock wall to the summit cairn. Continue along the crest for about 200m, turn right and drop down sharply to the wall gap. Bear left to Llyn Cwm y Foel, cross the fractured dam and head east to the south shore of the tarns, Llynnau Diffwys. Bear right to the track, turn left to Rhosydd Quarry (a playground for the mining historian)* and at the fork, keep right. After 150m, turn right, mount the incline between the spoil heaps and ascend to the open hillside. Then climb the long pathless slope to Moel yr Hydd, the second summit. Drop down due north to the fence, bear right to the track and turn right beside the lake, Llyn Cwmorthin. Cross the outflow by the bridge and at the T-junction, turn left. Pass through Cwmorthin Quarry,** bear right to the wall gap and ascend the tiresome ridge flank. Aim for the junction, pass through the gap and persevere upslope to the crest cairn. Turn left onto the path, poorly defined, ascend to the peat moor and bear right to the Allt Fawr summit cairn. Head north-west, drop down to the path and follow it to Moel Druman, the fourth summit. Continue along the path and after 300m, near the tarn, Llyn Coch, pick up the fence-line. This passes just below the penultimate summit, Ysgafell Wen (South), drops down to a sizeable pool and passes close to Ysgafell Wen (North), the sixth and final summit.

To return, head north-west for about 300m to the most northerly of the tarns, Llynnau'r Cŵn, bear left and follow the westerly outlet for 200m until it veers right. At this point, continue forward, drop down along the improving path and pass through the wall gaps. Go over the stile crossing the wall, pass through the deciduous wood and go through the gate. Turn left near the cottage, cross the bridge to the lane and turn right to the car park.

* Rhosydd Quarry was first worked for slate in a serious way in 1852. Employing about 200 men, its peak of production was reached in 1885. The quarry was shut down for the duration of the Great War with just two caretakers kept on but, soon after reopening, the owners went into liquidation. In July 1921, Rhosydd was purchased by the Colman mustard family who, a year earlier, had bought the Croes y Ddwy Afon Quarry the other side of Ffestiniog. After a few years of relative stability, markets for the slate began decreasing and production at Rhosydd was gradually run down. The quarry closed in September 1930.

** Cwmorthin Quarry opened in 1820, was achieving a respectable output by 1840 and by the early 1870s, employed over 300 men. Its history of industrial conflict was possibly the longest of any slate quarry in Wales. It was merged with the Oakeley Quarries in 1900.

ROUTE 34
A haven for the solitary rambler.

Group	Moelwyni
Number of summits	2
Time required	2¾ hours
Map	O.S. 1:25 000 Outdoor Leisure Sheet 18
Start	At 706443 — Cae Clyd car park, Ffestiniog
Parking	Car park at the start
Nearest centre	Blaenau Ffestiniog

1st Summit   99 MANOD MAWR (SOUTH)
                661m   **723446**
                Carries a trig pillar and a stone shelter.

2nd Summit   103 MANOD MAWR (NORTH)
                658m   **727458**
                Marked by a cairn.

From the car park, turn right onto the road, pass through the gate and continue along the track. Near the homestead, Bron Manod, bear left at the fork and approaching the barn, turn right. Cross the field, pass through the gate and beyond the next gate, bear left. Pass through the wall gap and two more gates, turn left by the stream and head upslope beside the wall. Pass through the gate and continue beside the fence. Where the lake comes into view, bear right, ascend to the path and follow it until level with the south shore. Then turn right and climb the rocky mountainside to the first summit, Manod Mawr (South). Drop down due north, slowly move right and aim for the conspicuous tarn, Llyn Pysgod. Turn right onto the quarry road and after 150m, turn left onto the ascending track to Manod Mawr (North), the second summit.

To return, rejoin the quarry road and about 200m past Llyn Pysgod, bear left down the incline to the derelict buildings (part of the old Graig Ddu Quarry).* Bear left at the fork, follow the path and walk back to the car park.

* Graig Ddu, the highest slate quarry in Wales, opened in 1840. In the early 1860s, a tramway in a series of inclines was built from the quarry down to the road at Bethania. The men descended in small one wheel and roller devices known as 'wild cars'. Fitted with a crude braking system, the cars hurtled down the inclines at speeds risked entirely by their occupants. The intrepid took a mere two minutes to complete the descent, the cautious nearer to five. The quarry reached its peak of production in 1873, employing about 100 men.

ROUTE 35

A watchful walk on beckoning hills. More demanding than the time suggests.

Group	Moelwyni
Number of summits	2
Time required	1¾ hours
Map	O.S. 1:25 000 Outdoor Leisure Sheet 18
Start	At 698485 — the junction of the A470 and the Aberconwy-Meirionnydd district boundary
Parking	Parking area at the junction
Nearest centre	Blaenau Ffestiniog (3km)

1st Summit 161 MOEL FARLWYD
577m   **707486**
Marked by a cairn.

2nd Summit 128 MOEL PENAMNEN
623m   **716483**
Marked by a cairn.

From the parking area, cross the road to the sheepfold and follow the sharply rising fence. Cross the stile to gain the first summit, Moel Farlwyd, recross the stile and turn left. Drop down beside the fence to the tarns, Llynnau Barlwyd, keep roughly in line with the fence and ascend between the craggy bluffs. Where the fence turns left, continue forward 100m, turn right onto the faint path and follow it to the second summit, Moel Penamnen.

To return, go back along the path for about 200m, turn left and drop down sharply to the obsolete dam between the tarns. Cross the dam, turn left and take the improving path back to the road.

ROUTE 36

A sobering adventure to the 'land of a thousand bogs'. For experienced walkers.

Group	Moelwyni
Number of summits	2
Time required	4½ hours
Map	O.S. 1:25 000 Outdoor Leisure Sheet 17
Start	At 627506 — Pont Bethania car park
Parking	Car park at the start
Nearest centre	Beddgelert (5km)

1st Summit   **145 MOEL MEIRCH**
                    607m   **661503**
                    The highest point is unmarked.

2nd Summit   **157 YR ARDDU**
                    589m   **673507**
                    Marked by a cairn.

From the car park, follow the road south for 400m, turn left onto the lane and go over the bridge spanning the river, the Afon Glaslyn. Pass through the gates to the turn in the lane, mount the track signed 'Edno' and drop down gently with the conifers to the left. Turn left at the junction and cross the stiles towards the homestead, Hafodydd Brithion. Bear right onto the path, pass through the gaps and go over the stile crossing the wall. Turn left, follow the path into the shallow gorge and continue beside the tumbling river, the Afon Llyn Edno. The path eventually crosses the river, passes through another gap and rises steadily to the valley head, where the landscape to the east is revealed. About 40m short of the cairn, bear left, pick up the faint path and ascend to the first summit, Moel Meirch. Drop down south-east, pass through the fence-line and cross Cwm Edno to the saddle. Bear left onto the ridge crest and traverse the sodden terrain to Yr Arddu, the second summit.

To return, go back to the valley head, prominent at the Edno watershed, pass the cairn and walk back to the car park.

ROUTE 37

Explores wet and featureless moorland. Do not attempt unless competent with map and compass.

Group	Moelwyni
Number of summits	1
Time required	2 hours
Map	O.S. 1:25 000 Outdoor Leisure Sheet 17
Start	At 659555 — the layby about 300m south of the Pen y Gwryd Hotel*
Parking	Layby at the start
Nearest centre	Llanberis (11km)

The Summit 155 CARNEDD Y CRIBAU
      591m   **676536**
      Marked by a cairn.

Opposite the layby, cross the stile, bear right and ascend beneath the power lines. Where the incline of the slope eases and the saturated moor unfolds, keep south-east, traverse the moor and eventually mount the slope of outcropping rock. Beyond another morass, pass between more rocks, go over the stile crossing the fence and make the short pull to the summit.

Return by the same route.

* Pen y Gwryd, originally a small early nineteenth century ale-house, modernised in 1847, is now the most famous climbing hotel in Wales. It was the training base of the successful 1953 Everest expedition and in October of that year, the hotel's Everest Room was officially opened by the expedition leader, John Hunt (now Lord Hunt). The ceiling of the room was autographed by the expedition members. The hotel stands on the northern perimeter of the only Roman marching camp identified in North Wales, the remains of which can still be seen.

ROUTE 38

Crosses some of Britain's oldest fossiliferous rocks (early Palaeozoic, 500-600 million years old). For experienced walkers.

Group	Rhinog
Number of summits	3
Time required	6 hours
Map	O.S. 1:25 000 Outdoor Leisure Sheet 18
Start	At 641269 — Maes y Garnedd Farmhouse*
Parking	Parking area near the farmhouse (fee)
Nearest centre	Harlech (13km)

1st Summit 69 RHINOG FACH
712m   664270
Marked by a cairn.

2nd Summit 50 Y LLETHR
756m   661257
Marked by a cairn.

3rd Summit 53 DIFFWYS
750m   661234
Carries a trig pillar and the remains of an ancient burial cairn. The cairn has been heavily robbed of material for the construction of the wall.

From the parking area, cross the stream, pass through the wall gate and follow the path into the rugged defile, Bwlch Drws Ardudwy. At the next gate, observe the location of the distant cairn, set up on a heathery knoll. Keep to the path and on reaching the knoll, cross the boulder in the wall, mount the steep path and make headway up the mountainside. The path eventually gains a plateau, bends right and rises again to the first summit, Rhinog Fach. From here, head east to the wall junction, turn right onto the path and drop down sharply beside the wall to the saddle above Llyn Hywel.** Beyond the saddle, the path, avoiding the rock bluffs, moves temporarily away from the wall, climbs the scree-covered slope and leads to Y Llethr, the second summit. Continue to follow the wall (a classic example of the skill of drystone walling), cross the stile and traverse the crest of the long undulating ridge, Crib y Rhiw. Go over the stile crossing the wall, turn right and ascend to Diffwys, the third and final summit.

To return, cross the summit stile and head just north of west for about 400m. Descend the steep grass couloir and progress to the sharp bend in the reservoir access road. After about 700m, near a prominent erratic boulder, turn right onto the rising track and shortly, where the track bends right, bear left onto the faint path. Go over the stile crossing the wall, pass through the gap and follow the path. Pass through the wall gate, turn right onto the road and walk back to the farmhouse.

* Maes y Garnedd, the remote but well known farmhouse, was the birthplace and ancestral home of Colonel John Jones, husband of Oliver Cromwell's sister, Catherine. In 1648, he was one of the judges at Westminster Hall who found Charles I guilty of treason, a verdict leading to the King's execution in January 1649. In gratitude, Cromwell later appointed Jones Parliamentary Commissioner for the Government of Ireland. As Lord Protector of England from 1653 until his death in 1658, Cromwell ruled virtually as king. At the Restoration in 1660, Jones was executed along with nine other regicides, meeting his death with commendable courage.

** Llyn Hywel, guarded menacingly by glacier-smoothed slabs, is arguably the best situated tarn in Wales. During his visit to this area in 1188, Giraldus Cambrensis (Gerald of Wales) noted that within the tarn's mysterious depths, lurked monocular fish — a claim, however, that is still to be substantiated. (Cambrensis, the famous cleric and chronicler, was related to several Welsh princes including Rhys ap Tewdwr and the Lord Rhys.)

ROUTE 39

Ventures into bleak and rugged country. For experienced walkers.

Group	Rhinog
Number of summits	1
Time required	3 hours
Map	O.S. 1:25 000 Outdoor Leisure Sheet 18
Start	At 646314 — Cwm Bychan car park
Parking	Car park at the start (fee)
Nearest centre	Harlech (10km)

The Summit 65 RHINOG FAWR
720m   **656290**
One of the great rock peaks of Wales. The summit sports a trig pillar, a stone shelter and several cairns.

From the car park entrance, turn right and take the path opposite the barn. The path crosses a causeway, passes through a deciduous wood and leads to the Roman Steps.* After about 600m, pass through the wall gap to enter the nature reserve,** turn right onto the path and ascend sharply beside the wall. Where the incline of the slope eases, the path bends left and near the tarn, Llyn Du, steering clear of the rock bluff, turns right and forks. At this point, bear left away from the wall and at the next fork, overlooking a secluded pool, bear right onto the ascending scree path to the summit.

Return by the same route.

* The Roman Steps, the mysterious stairway of flat unhewn slabs, may be attributable, despite its name, to medieval industry. The well-engineered path which penetrates the desolate pass, Bwlch Tyddiad, was probably laid down as a part of the packhorse trading route between Bala and the coast, long after the legions departed. It is likely that the pass was first exploited in prehistoric times, creating a path consolidated later by the Romans. Their auxiliary fort, at nearby Tomen y Mur, was occupied until about AD 140.

** Rhinog National Nature Reserve, established in 1958, covers an area of highly inaccessible mountainous country. The higher crags provide a breeding place for ravens, ring ouzels and wrens, while the lower rocks and slopes are a haven for meadow pipits and wheatears. A herd of feral goats may be spotted on the reserve.

ROUTE 40

A bliss for those wishing to elude the company of their fellow beings. One demanding slope and some wet patches.

Group	Rhinog
Number of summits	1
Time required	1¾ hours
Map	O.S. 1:25 000 Outdoor Leisure Sheet 18
Start	At 713217 — the end of Pant Llwyfog Road, Llanelltud
Parking	Limited roadside at the start
Nearest centre	Dolgellau (5km)

The Summit 125 Y GARN
           629m   **702230**
           A wild outpost. Marked by a cairn.

At the end of the road, pass through the gates and follow the track to the homestead, Blaen-y-cwm, where a complex wall system is encountered. Pass through the gap and continue along the track. Just short of the next gap, ascend left, pass through the wider gap and bear right. Pass through more gaps towards the forest, bear left across the steep grassland and ascend to the junction. Cross the stile in the wall, pass the sheepfold and continue upslope with the wall to the right. Where the wall turns left, pass through the gap and ascend to the summit.

Return by the same route.

ROUTE 41

A mountain walker's paradise. The going is hard; do not attempt unless in good shape.

Group	Rhinog
Number of summits	2
Time required	3½ hours
Map	O.S. 1:25 000 Outdoor Leisure Sheet 18
Start	At 646314 — Cwm Bychan car park
Parking	Car park at the start (fee)
Nearest centre	Harlech (10km)

1st Summit **153 CLIP**
596m   **656331**
Marked by a cairn.

2nd Summit **129 MOEL YSGAFARNOGOD**
623m   **658345**
Carries a trig pillar and a rudimentary stone shelter.

From the car park entrance, turn right and pass through the gate next to the barn. Bear right onto the ascending path, pass through the wall gaps to the valley head and turn left onto the steep path which higher up bends right below the col, Bwlch Gwilym. Where the path begins to descend, turn left and make the short pull to Clip, the first summit. Rejoin the path, head north past the pools and after a glimpse of the tarn, Llyn Corn Ystwc, cross the pavement of striated slabs. Continue along the path and make headway past the tarn, Llyn Du. Scramble down the low rock terrace, press on north across the difficult terrain and ascend sharply to the second summit, Moel Ysgafarnogod.

To return, head just south of east, descend to the wall and pass through the gap. Continue forward 30m, turn right and drop down roughly in line with the wall. At the junction, cross the stream to the path, turn right to the fork and bear right to the car park.

ROUTE 42

Follows the course once taken by the drovers and the London to Harlech mail coach. Can be attempted by energetic casual walkers.

Group	Rhinog
Number of summits	1
Time required	2¼ hours
Map	O.S. 1:25 000 Outdoor Leisure Sheet 18
Start	At 633259 — Cilcochwyn Farmhouse
Parking	Parking area at the farmhouse (fee)
Nearest centre	Harlech (11km)

The Summit 158 MOELFRE
588m   **626245**

A lone sentinel guarding the oldest mountain mass in Wales. The ancient summit cairn, legend states, marks the burial place of the warrior, Moel, who died while climbing the hill. It was from the top that King Arthur threw one of his famous quoits, which landed near Pont Fadog. The capstone of a burial chamber there is known locally, as a result of the story, as Arthur's Quoit.

From the farmhouse, head west along the road and after 300m, turn left onto the path (the way the drovers and eighteenth century coach would have gone). Pass through the gate, continue along the path and pass through the wall gap. The path rises steadily, passes through another gap and leads to a stile crossing a wall. (From here, the drovers and coach would have continued south to the bridge, Pont Scethin.) Cross the stile, turn right beside the wall and ascend to the boulder field where, over the wall, the summit cairn appears. Drop down with the wall, go over the stile crossing it and proceed to the cairn.

Return by the same route.

ROUTE 43

An easy trip into seldom-trodden country. Some boggy patches.

Group	Rhinog
Number of summits	1
Time required	1½ hours
Map	O.S. 1:25 000 Outdoor Leisure Sheet 18
Start	At 684358 — the road-path junction near Ty'n Twll smallholding
Parking	Limited roadside at the junction
Nearest centre	Blaenau Ffestiniog (18km)

The Summit 174 MOEL Y GRIAFOLEN
                  535m   **672352**
A fine vantage-point for Llyn Trawsfynydd* and Trawsfynydd Power Station.**

From the road, pass through the smaller of the gates beneath the power lines, follow the path and pass through more gates. Continue beside the wall, pass the lone tree and progress to the junction. Pass through the gate, turn left and pass through the wall gap. Then head due south away from the wall and climb the terraced heather slope to the summit cairn.

Return by the same route.

* Llyn Trawsfynydd, an artificial lake, was formed between 1924 and 1928 by damming the Afonydd Llenyrch and Prysor and flooding a large tract of swampland known as Cors Goch (Red Bog). It was created to supply water to Maentwrog Power Station. In preparation for the opening of Trawsfynydd Power Station, the lake was drained to allow the bund walls to be extended to connect the islands. This was to establish an unbroken circular water flow from the station cooling outlet, which releases the warm water after its use, round the lake back to the inlet — a five-and-a-half day cycle.

** Trawsfynydd Power Station, designed by Sir Basil Spence, commenced operations in January 1965 when the first of the four turbo-alternators supplied electricity to the national grid. Two months later, maximum output was reached when the fourth alternator came into operation. Trawsfynydd was the first nuclear power station in Britain to be built inland and the first to use a lake for cooling purposes. It was officially opened in October 1968 by the Rt. Hon. James Griffiths, Secretary of State for Wales, 1964-66.

ROUTE 44

A touching and unforgettable pilgrimage. For experienced walkers.

Group	Arennig
Number of summits	2
Time required	4½ hours
Map	O.S. 1:25 000 Outdoor Leisure Sheet 18
Start	At 816394 — the junction of the A4212 and the B4391
Parking	Parking area at the junction
Nearest centre	Bala (13km)

1st Summit   24 ARENNIG FAWR
854m   **826369**

Carries a trig pillar, an ancient burial cairn and a slate memorial plaque. The cairn has been mutilated by the incorporation of a shelter. The plaque commemorates the death of eight American airmen whose Boeing B-17 Flying Fortress bomber flew into the summit in August 1943.

2nd Summit   52 MOEL LLYFNANT
751m   **808351**

Marked by a cairn.

From the junction, follow the lane signed 'Arennig' and after 600m, near the power lines, turn right onto the track. Cross the cattle grid, pass through the gates and continue along the track. At the derelict farmhouse, Amnodd Wen, turn left off the track and ascend roughly in line with the stream. After 400m, near the stream, pass through the wall gap and climb the long and trying mountainside, littered with fragments of aircraft remains, to the first summit, Arennig Fawr. From here, head south beside the fence-line, slowly move right and drop down to the junction of the wall and the track deserted earlier. Head east to the far end of the collapsed wall, bear left and ascend sharply to the second summit, Moel Llyfnant.

To return, descend due north where soon, at the edge of the forest near the homestead, Amnodd Bwll, a track junction comes into view. Take the track leading north-west, pass through the gate and progress through the forest. On reaching the A4212, turn right and walk back to the junction.

ROUTE 45

A break from twentieth century pressures. One stiff slope. Can be attempted by fit novice walkers.

Group	Arennig
Number of summits	1
Time required	3¼ hours
Map	O.S. 1:25 000 Outdoor Leisure Sheet 23
Start	At 796222 — the road junction 600m north of Hengwrt Hall School entrance
Parking	Limited roadside at the junction
Nearest centre	Dolgellau (9km)

The Summit 60 RHOBELL FAWR
         734m   **786256**
         Sports a trig pillar and a cairn.

From the junction, take the road leading north and in due course, pass through the gate, bear left at the fork and follow the track. Pass the homestead, Cae'r Defaid, progress into the forest and at the T-junction, turn left. At the forest edge, pass through the gate, cross the stream and head north to the path. Turn left, pass through the gate and shortly, where the path begins to descend, bear right and cross the boulder slope to the wall. Ascend to the junction, turn right and pass through the gap to the summit.

Return by the same route.

ROUTE 46

Into wild and obscure territory. In mist, the proficient use of map and compass will be essential.

Group	Arennig
Number of summits	1
Time required	2 hours
Map	O.S. 1:25 000 Outdoor Leisure Sheet 18
Start	At 816394 — the junction of the A4212 and the B4391
Parking	Parking area at the junction
Nearest centre	Bala (13km)

The Summit 79 ARENNIG FACH
689m   **820415**

Carries a trig pillar, a stone shelter and the remains of an ancient burial cairn. The cairn has been robbed of material for the construction of the shelter.

Opposite the parking area, pass through the gate, turn right and ascend beneath the power lines. Keep north to the sheepfold, turn right and continue beside the fence. After about 150m, step over the fence, cross the stream and progress just east of north. Then climb the long featureless slope to the summit.

Return by the same route.

ROUTE 47

A lonely walk on mysterious hills.

Group	Arennig
Number of summits	2
Time required	4 hours
Map	O.S. 1:25 000 Outdoor Leisure Sheet 18
Start	At 848413 — the layby near Capel Celyn Memorial Chapel*
Parking	Layby at the start
Nearest centre	Bala (10km)

1st Summit   **113 CARNEDD LLECHWEDD LLYFN**
643m   **857444**
The highest point is unmarked. The cairn-marked spur to the south-east is 3m lower.

2nd Summit   **92 CARNEDD Y FILIAST**
669m   **871445**
Carries a trig pillar, an ancient burial cairn and a nineteenth century boundary stone. The cairn has been mutilated by the incorporation of a shelter. The stone, sepulchral in appearance, inscribed with the letters CD on one side and TI on the other, once marked the boundary between the parishes of Cerrigydrudion and Tir Ifan. (Tir Ifan has since been incorporated in the parish of Tir Eidda.) The summit is the meeting place of six current administrative boundaries.

From the layby, follow the road east for about 250m, turn left onto the track and pass through the gate. After 200m, leave the track, pass through the gate and follow the path beside the wall. Pass beneath the power lines, keep to the right of the sheepfold and continue beside the wall. After about 350m, where the wall begins to descend, bear right onto the vestigial track which follows the course of the stream, the Nant Tynant, pass through the fence gate and continue forward. Pass through the gates, turn left and progress beside the rising fence. Where the fence turns left, continue forward and ascend to Carnedd Llechwedd Llyfn, the first summit. Drop down north-east to the fence and follow it to the second summit, Carnedd y Filiast.

To return, descend due east to the track, turn right and eventually cross the stream, the Nant y Coed. Turn right at the T-junction, continue along the track and drop down to the forest edge. Follow the path through the forest, turn right onto the A4212 and walk back to the layby.

* The Chapel commemorates the hamlet of Capel Celyn, submerged in the early 1960s when part of the valley of the Afon Tryweryn was flooded to form Celyn Reservoir. Created to supply water to Liverpool, the reservoir was officially opened in October 1965 by Alderman Frank Cain, Chairman of Liverpool Water Committee. It has a maximum depth of 43m. Also submerged was the homestead, Hafod Fadog, once the meeting place of the valley's tightly-knit Quaker community. In the seventeenth and eighteenth centuries, driven from their homes by persecution, over half of the community fled to Pennsylvania, the Quaker haven founded in 1682 by William Penn, the devout English Quaker. (Penn was imprisoned in the Tower for his beliefs in 1668 and it was there he wrote the acclaimed book on Quaker practice, *No Cross, No Crown.*) During the extraordinary drought of summer 1976, the reservoir's water level dropped significantly and the remains of Capel Celyn were clearly revealed.

ROUTE 48

An easily followed ramble with something to please everyone. A challenging opportunity for fit family groups.

Group	Arennig
Number of summits	1
Time required	4¼ hours
Map	O.S. 1:25 000 Outdoor Leisure Sheet 23
Start	At 796222 — the road junction 600m north of Hengwrt Hall School entrance
Parking	Limited roadside at the junction
Nearest centre	Dolgellau (9km)

The Summit 98 Y DDUALLT
　　　　　662m　　　　　　　　　　　　　　　**810273**
　　　　　Marked by a cairn.

From the junction, take the road leading north and in due course, pass through the gate, keep right at the fork and pass through more gates. Make headway into the forest, continue along the track and after about 3km, where the track begins to descend, turn right onto the firebreak. Turn left at the T-junction and at the fork, bear right to the forest edge. Turn right beside the fence, ascend to the junction and turn right to the summit cairn.

Return by the same route.

ROUTE 49

Secures a remote 600m summit with relatively little effort. Unsuitable for families with young children.

Group	Arennig
Number of summits	1
Time required	1 hour
Map	O.S. 1:25 000 Outdoor Leisure Sheet 18
Start	At 779334 — the eastern edge of the Coed y Brenin forestry block
Parking	Limited roadside 25m east of the cattle grid
Nearest centre	Bala (18km)

The Summit 132 FOEL BOETH
619m   **778344**
The highest point, just east of the fence, is unmarked.

From the road, head north beside the wall and ascend beside the forest perimeter. After about 300m, near the sheepfold, bear right away from the forest, continue upslope and progress to the fence junction which comes into view. Then continue forward beside the fence the short distance to the summit.

Return by the same route.

ROUTE 50

A peaceful walk with nature as your only companion.

Group	Arennig
Number of summits	1
Time required	2 hours
Map	O.S. 1:25 000 Outdoor Leisure Sheet 18
Start	At 966446 — Llangwm village centre
Parking	Limited roadside in the village
Nearest centre	Corwen (13km)

The Summit 140 FOEL GOCH
611m   **953422**

Carries a trig pillar, a cairn and a nineteenth century boundary stone. The stone, sepulchral in appearance, once marked the boundary between the parishes of Llangwm and Llanfor. (Llanfor has since been incorporated in the parish of Llandderfel.)

From the village centre, head west to Groes Chapel, turn left onto the lane and pass through the gates. Pass the entrance to Ceseilgwm Farmhouse, bear right onto the track and ascend beside the trees. Pass through the gate, continue beside the fence and progress to the junction. Pass through the gate, turn right off the track and cross the stile in the fence. Then bear left and climb to the summit.

Return by the same route.

ROUTE 51

An arduous walk on distant hills.

Group	Berwyn
Number of summits	3
Time required	5¾ hours
Map	O.S. 1:50 000 Landranger Sheet 125
Start	At 035371 — Llandrillo car park
Parking	Car park at the start
Nearest centre	Corwen (8km)

1st Summit **42 CADAIR FRONWEN**
785m **077346**

Carries an ancient burial cairn mutilated by the construction of a modern cairn. Bwrdd Arthur (King Arthur's Table), named on the map, probably refers to the table-like boulder 10m to the south and not to the original cairn, itself once table-like.

2nd Summit **28 CADAIR BERWYN**
830m **071323**

The highest point is unmarked and not obvious. The ancient sepulchral mound to the north, surmounted by a trig pillar, is 3m lower. It is this point of the ridge to which the peak's name refers.

3rd Summit **29 MOEL SYCH**
827m **066318**

Carries the remains of an ancient burial cairn. The summit coincides with the Clwyd-Powys county boundary.

Opposite the car park entrance, take the road leading south (Berwyn Street) and at the end, follow the track. Pass through the gate, follow the path beside the wall and note the location of the small isolated forestry block. The path, tenuous at times, eventually leads to a fence gate, passes the forestry block and forks. At this point, bear left, progress upslope and cross the traversing path to the fence. Turn right to Cadair Fronwen, the first summit, head south beside the fence and drop down to the pass, Bwlch Maen Gwynedd. Ascend to the junction, pass through the gate and turn right to the second summit, Cadair Berwyn. Then continue beside the fence to the third and final summit, Moel Sych.

To return, head due north for about 1km to the crest of the ridge, Foel Fawr, turn left to the fence and descend to the junction. Pass through the gate, turn right towards the sheepfold and cross the stream, the Nant Cwm Tywyll. Continue forward, pass through the gate and continue forward again. At the junction, pass through the gate, turn left and walk back to the car park.

ROUTE 52

A modest ridge walk above rich pastoral land. Can be attempted by fit novice walkers.

Group	Berwyn
Number of summits	3
Time required	3½ hours
Map	O.S. 1:50 000 Landranger Sheet 125
Start	At 118306 — the bridge, Bont Wen (not named on the map)
Parking	Limited roadside by the bridge
Nearest centre	Llangollen (19km)

1st Summit   **83 MYNYDD TARW**
                681m   **112324**
                Crowned by an ancient burial cairn mutilated by the incorporation of a shooting box.

2nd Summit   **77 FOEL WEN**
                691m   **099334**
                The highest point, just north of the fence, is unmarked.

3rd Summit   **56 TOMLE**
                742m   **085335**
                Marked by a cairn.

From the bridge, head north to the telephone box, turn right and follow the farm track. Just past the third farmyard, Votty, pass through the gate to enter the forest, follow the path and progress upslope. Near the forest edge, leave the path which at this point turns right, continue forward and ascend beside the fence to Mynydd Tarw, the first summit. Follow the fence leading west and at the junction, bear right to the second summit, Foel Wen. Continue beside the fence to the third and final summit, Tomle.

To return, drop down south, pass the quartz shepherds' cairn and go through the fence gate. Turn left onto the track and walk back to the bridge.

ROUTE 53

An escapade through a wilderness of heather. Snail's pace headway across several stretches. For experienced walkers.

Group	Berwyn
Number of summits	3
Time required	3¾ hours
Map	O.S. 1:25 000 Outdoor Leisure Sheet 23
Start	At 958255 — the bridge, Bont yr Henrhyd (not named on the map)
Parking	Parking area by the bridge
Nearest centre	Bala (13km)

1st Summit   **138 CEFN GWYNTOG**
                 615m   **976266**
                 Marked by an upright stone.

2nd Summit   **94 CYRNIAU NOD**
                 667m   **988279**
                 A forgotten outpost. Marked by a cairn.

3rd Summit   **121 STAC RHOS**
                 630m   **968278**
                 A summit of little appeal. Unmarked.

From the parking area, ascend due north towards the fence and after 150m, turn right onto the traversing path. Pass the lone boulder to the forest corner, pass through the gate and follow the path beside the fence. At the next corner, turn right, cross the streams and keep beside the fence. Where the fence turns right, continue forward and climb the difficult heather slope to the first summit, Cefn Gwyntog. Drop down north-east, persevere across the bleak moorland waste and ascend to the second summit, Cyrniau Nod. Head north to the junction, turn left and follow the fence to the third and final summit, Stac Rhos.

To return, head south to the forest edge, pick up the path and walk back to the bridge.

ROUTE 54

A ramble where travellers should not be troubled with any company other than their own. In mist, the proficient use of map and compass will be essential.

Group	Berwyn
Number of summits	1
Time required	2 hours
Map	O.S. 1:50 000 Landranger Sheet 125
Start	At 019300 — the small parking area on the west side of Milltir Gerrig Pass
Parking	Parking area at the start
Nearest centre	Bala (15km)

The Summit 109 FOEL CWM SIAN LWYD
648m   **995313**

Crowned by an ancient sepulchral mound surmounted by a trig pillar. The ancient burial cairn to the north, mutilated by the incorporation of a shooting box, is the conspicuous structure catching the eye while travelling south along the B4391 from Bala.

From the parking area, mount the descending track and cross the stile next to the gate. Bear right at the fork, cross the stile and continue beside the stream. After 150m, cross the stream, pass through the gate and turn right beside the fence. At the junction, pass through the gate onto the track, traverse the moor to the fence and cross the stile. Keep to the track, now less distinct, continue upslope and after about 500m, bear right to the summit.

Return by the same route.

ROUTE 55

A walk of distinction. Safe and easily followed. Ideal for fit family groups.

Group	Berwyn
Number of summits	1
Time required	4½ hours
Map	O.S. 1:50 000 Landranger Sheet 125
Start	At 056411 — Cynwyd village centre
Parking	Limited roadside in the village
Nearest centre	Corwen (4km)

The Summit 120 MOEL FFERNA
630m   116397
Carries an ancient burial cairn mutilated by the incorporation of a shelter. In the early nineteenth century, an enlarged food vessel containing a cremation was found beneath the cairn.

From the village centre, take the road leading east (Waterfall Road) and make headway to the old foresters' lodge of Celyncoed Isaf (not named on the map). Keep right at the fork, continue along the access road and at the next fork, keep right again. At the next fork, bear left onto the ascending road, progress to the forest edge and pass through the gate. Follow the track across the moor and on reaching the gate, turn left beside the fence, ascend to the junction and cross the stile to the summit.

Return by the same route.

ROUTE 56

A steady plod where the starting point is always in view.

Group	Berwyn
Number of summits	1
Time required	¾ hour
Map	O.S. 1:25 000 Outdoor Leisure Sheet 23
Start	At 946273 — the head of Cwm Hirnant
Parking	Small parking area at the start
Nearest centre	Bala (11km)

The Summit 126 FOEL Y GEIFR
626m   **937275**
Carries a trig pillar.

From the parking area, drop down due west, cross the stile in the fence and follow the rising vestigial track. Approaching the ridge crest, bear left off the track, continue upslope and ascend to the trig.

Return by the same route.

ROUTE 57

A saunter from Wales's highest car park.

Group	Berwyn
Number of summits	1
Time required	1 hour
Map	O.S. 1:25 000 Outdoor Leisure Sheet 23
Start	At 913232 — Bwlch y Groes car park
Parking	Car park at the start
Nearest centre	Bala (17km)

The Summit 127 MOEL Y CERRIG DUON
625m   **923241**
The principal watershed of Wales. The summit is a vantage-point for Llyn Fyrnwy.*

From the car park, cross the cattle grid and head upslope with the fence to the right. At the junction, the site of a seismological data transmission mast, turn left and continue beside the fence to the summit cairn.

Return by the same route.

* Llyn Fyrnwy, the largest Victorian man-made lake in Wales, boasts a perimeter of 18km and a capacity of 57 000 megalitres. The lake was created to supply water to Liverpool by flooding the valley of the infant Afon Fyrnwy. The gothic straining tower on the north-east shore is the start of the 109km aqueduct. Construction work began in 1881 and five years later, at its peak, the labour force had exceeded 1000. In November 1888, the valves in the dam were closed and nearly one year later the lake was full. On completion of the first instalment of the aqueduct, the first water reached Liverpool in July 1892. During the 1974 reorganisation of the water industry, the Severn-Trent Water Authority took over the guardianship of the lake from the Liverpool Corporation.

ROUTE 58

A tough but rewarding excursion into territory where, sadly, antagonism between landowners and walkers has led to public access being curtailed.

Access to the summits of the route is using courtesy paths created by an agreement, subject to a yearly review, between the landowners and the Snowdonia National Park Authority.

Group	Aran
Number of summits	2
Time required	5¾ hours
Map	O.S. 1:25 000 Outdoor Leisure Sheet 23
Start	At 853184 — the north end of Fawnog Fawr Common
Parking	Limited roadside at the start
Nearest centre	Dolgellau (19km)

1st Summit   **16 ARAN FAWDDWY**
               905m   **862223**
               The highest mountain in Wales south of Yr Wyddfa (Snowdon). The summit carries a trig pillar superimposed on a large pile of stones, possibly the remains of a Bronze Age burial cairn.

2nd Summit   **20 ARAN BENLLYN**
               885m   **867243**
               Marked by a cairn.

From the common, head north along the lane and after 250m, cross the bridge spanning the river, the Afon Cywarch. Follow the path, cross the stiles and continue along the track. Cross the stream, mount the hill path and ascend across the flank of the valley, Hengwm. The path eventually leads to the start of a courtesy path where there is a quartz cairn and an information board. The courtesy path circles the valley head in line with the fence and after crossing the spur, Drysgol, where there is a fence junction, leads to the Drws Bach cairn.* From here, ascend beside the fence to the courtesy path junction, cross the stiles and turn right to the first summit, Aran Fawddwy. Drop down north, cross the stile and continue along the path which, beyond more stiles, leads to the second summit, Aran Benllyn.

To return, go back to the courtesy path junction, ignore the stiles and head downslope with the fence to the left. At Waun Camddwr, the boggy plateau, cross the stiles and keep south-west beside the fence. Where the fence veers right, continue forward, pass the pool to the information board and turn left beside the fence. Where the fence ends near a lone tree, keep the cascading stream to the right, drop down into the gorge and cross the single handrail bridge. Follow the path, cross the stile and turn right onto the track. Pass Blaen Cywarch Farmhouse, go through the gate onto the lane and walk back to the common.

* The cairn was erected by the RAF St Athan Mountain Rescue Team in memory of their colleague, Michael Aspain. He was killed by lightning here in June 1960 while on duty with them. The life of another team member was probably saved by the level-headedness of Flying Officer Michael Davies, deputy in charge, who applied artificial respiration at once. The base of the cairn, of Devonian age rocks in Ordovician country, was brought from Pen y Fan, the highest mountain in the team's area of responsibility.

ROUTE 59

Encompasses a unique and dramatic landscape. For experienced walkers.

Group	Cadair Idris
Number of summits	4
Time required	4½ hours
Map	O.S. 1:25 000 Outdoor Leisure Sheet 23
Start	At 732115 — Dôl Idris car park
Parking	Car park at the start
Nearest centre	Dolgellau (12km)

1st Summit **41 MYNYDD PENCOED**
791m   **710121**
Also known as Craig Cau. The highest point, just north of the stile, is unmarked.

2nd Summit **32 CYFRWY**
811m   **703133**
Carries a stone shelter.

3rd Summit **18 PEN Y GADAIR**
893m   **711130**
Carries a trig pillar and a refuge hut. The hut is the restored remains of the refreshment cabin erected here in the 1830s — a time when Pen y Gadair was thought by many to be the highest peak in Wales. The cabin was built by the Dolgellau mountain guide, David Pugh, whose son Robert, also a guide, once scaled the peak four times in one day.

4th Summit **23 MYNYDD MOEL**
863m   **727136**
Carries a stone shelter.

To the rear of the car park toilet block, pass through the gate onto the drive, turn right and pass the entrance to Dôl y Cae (once the home of the renowned lexicographer, Dr Owen Pugh). Cross the bridge, pass through the gate to enter the nature reserve* and mount the stairway of the Minffordd Path (named after the former farmhouse now a hotel). Ascend through the wood, pass through the wall gate and follow the path. On reaching the large junction cairn, bear left at the fork and continue upslope. The path, never exposed, climbs steadily along the jagged crest of the vast amphitheatre and leads to the first summit, Mynydd Pencoed. Cross the stile, drop down along the path and after about 600m, where the path bends right, continue forward. Ascend due north to the track (an old pony trail), turn left and at the fork, bear right to Cyfrwy, the second summit. Go back to the fork and follow the track east to Pen y Gadair, the third summit. Continue east, traverse the scarp crest to the fence and cross the stile to the fourth and final summit, Mynydd Moel.

To return, drop down beside the fence, cross the stiles and pass through the wall gap. Cross the next stile, follow the path away from the fence and cross the stream to the Minffordd Path. Turn left and walk back to the car park.

* Cadair Idris National Nature Reserve, established in 1955 and bought by the Nature Conservancy Council in 1976, preserves an area of foremost geomorphological, botanical and ornithological importance. Fashioned by the movement of ice, the rocks of the landscape are Ordovician in age — a time of violent igneous activity. Cwm Cau, the centre-piece of the reserve, is possibly the best example of a cirque (rock basin) in Britain. Its formidable cliffs provide a suitable habitat for rare arctic-alpine plants and a breeding place for buzzards, merlins and ravens. The steep southern approach to the cwm (the Minffordd Path) is through an attractive wood of alder, ash, oak and rowan. (Oaks, native to the British Isles and their leaf the symbol of the National Trust, are sadly in decline because of acid rain pollution caused by coal-burning power stations and car exhaust poison.)

ROUTE 60

A fairly short but invigorating trip. One section of mild scrambling. Can be attempted by fit novice walkers.

Group	Cadair Idris
Number of summits	1
Time required	2 hours
Map	O.S. 1:25 000 Outdoor Leisure Sheet 23
Start	At 753135 — Bwlch Llyn Bach car park
Parking	Car park at the start
Nearest centre	Dolgellau (9km)

The Summit 82 GAU GRAIG
           683m   **744141**
           Marked by a cairn.

From the car park, follow the road north for about 600m, go over the stile crossing the fence and bear left to the ascending fence. Follow the path, pass through the gate and continue forward. Where the incline of the slope steepens, the path, seeking a way through the rock bluffs, moves away from the fence and soon peters out. At this point, scramble over the rocks, rejoin the fence to the summit ridge and turn right to the cairn.

Return by the same route.

ROUTE 61

A memorable odyssey. The slopes are toilsome; do not attempt unless in good shape.

Group	Cadair Idris
Number of summits	2
Time required	4½ hours
Map	O.S. 1:25 000 Outdoor Leisure Sheet 23
Start	At 671088 — Llanfihangel-y-Pennant car park
Parking	Car park at the start
Nearest centre	Tywyn (15km)

1st Summit **100 TYRAU MAWR**
661m   **676135**
The highest point, near the fence junction and stile, is unmarked.

2nd Summit **131 CRAIG Y LLYN**
622m   **665119**
The highest point, just north of the fence, is unmarked.

From the car park entrance, turn right, follow the lane and cross the bridge spanning the river, the Afon Cadair. Pass the Mary Jones Monument* to the farmhouse, Gwastadfryn, follow the track and pass through the gates. On reaching the sheepfolds at Hafoty Gwastadfryn (a former shepherds' lodge), continue north for about 350m, bear left at the fork and drop down along the track. Where the track ends, ascend due north, pass through the fence gate and cross the traversing track. Press on upslope to Tyrau Mawr, the first summit, cross the stile and continue forward beside the fence to the second summit, Craig y Llyn.

To return, drop down just north of east, pick up the track at Hafoty Gwastadfryn and walk back to the car park.

* The Mary Jones Monument was erected by the Sunday Schools of Merioneth. It commemorates a brave and determined girl, born in 1784 in the once picturesque cottage of Ty'n y Ddôl, in

the ruins of which the monument stands. At the age of ten, Mary started to save her pocket money to buy a Bible in Welsh,** a prized possession until the mid-nineteenth century. Six years later, having saved enough, she eagerly set off to obtain her copy. She walked barefoot to spare her shoes over mountain tracks to Bala, a distance of about 40km, only to discover the pastor there, Thomas Charles, had sold the last one. However, seeing her disappointment and the effort she had made, he gave her his own copy. So inspired by Mary's love for the Word of God and saddened by the shortage of Bibles in Welsh, Charles began a campaign which led to the beginning of the British and Foreign Bible Society. Later in her life, Mary moved to the nearby village of Bryn-crug and lived there in a cottage that is still occupied today. She died in December 1864 and her gravestone can be seen in the grounds of Bryn-crug's Bethlehem Chapel. (Thomas Charles was born in 1755 near Carmarthen and was educated at Jesus College, Oxford. He was an influential Methodist reformer and a pioneer of the Sunday School movement in Wales. His statue stands proudly outside Bala's Tegid Chapel.)

** The Bible's historic translation into Welsh was completed in 1588. It was the fruition of a self-imposed ten-year assignment undertaken by The Revd William Morgan in his vicarage at Llanrhaeadr-ym-Mochnant. His accomplishment prompted the Queen, Elizabeth I, to reward him with the prestigious bishopric of Llandaf, the oldest in Wales (the see was founded in the mid-sixth century). The translation formed the bedrock of modern Welsh literature and is the most important single contribution to the survival of the Welsh language, now the oldest in Europe. A copy is exhibited in the cathedral museum at St Asaph. Morgan was born in 1545 in a modest farmhouse in the secluded valley of the Wybrnant, near Penmachno. (The farmhouse, Tŷ Mawr, is now extensively restored and owned by the National Trust.) In 1565, he went to Cambridge where he took his Bachelor of Arts degree in 1567 and his Masters degree in 1571. He was ordained by the Bishop of Ely in 1568 and appointed vicar of St Dogfan's, Llanrhaeadr-ym-Mochnant in 1578. He was Bishop of St Asaph from 1601 until he died in 1604.

ROUTE 62

A bracing walk on brooding hills. The going is rough and the summits are shelterless.

Group	Dyfi Forest
Number of summits	3
Time required	3¾ hours
Map	O.S. 1:25 000 Outdoor Leisure Sheet 23
Start	At 802170 — Bwlch Oerddrws car park
Parking	Car park at the start
Nearest centre	Dolgellau (8km)

1st Summit **102 CRIBIN FAWR**
              659m   **794153**
              The highest point, near the fence junction, is unmarked.

2nd Summit **148 MYNYDD DOLGOED**
              605m   **801141**
              The highest point, near the fence junction, is unmarked.

3rd Summit **88 MAESGLASAU**
              674m   **822151**
              The highest point, just south of the fence, is unmarked.

Cross the car park stile, turn left and follow the fence. Where the fence turns left, continue forward, mount the path and progress upslope. Higher up, the path bends left back to the fence and leads to Cribin Fawr, the first summit. From here, head south-east and follow the fence to Mynydd Dolgoed, the second summit. Then head north-east, follow the fence along the Craig Portas escarpment and cross the stile. Turn left and continue beside the fence to the third and final summit, Maesglasau.

To return, head north-west and drop down the crest of the long curving ridge where there are traces of a path. Aim for the boulders, cross the stream beneath the trees and continue forward beside the fence. After 100m, turn right, cross the stream and pass beneath the power lines. Ascend to the gate, turn left onto the A470 and walk back to the car park.

ROUTE 63
A dream-land for the lone adventurer.

Group	Dyfi Forest
Number of summits	2
Time required	2¾ hours
Map	O.S. 1:25 000 Outdoor Leisure Sheet 23
Start	At 753135 — Bwlch Llyn Bach car park
Parking	Car park at the start
Nearest centre	Dolgellau (9km)

1st Summit   **147 MYNYDD CEISWYN**
                     605m   **772139**
                     The highest point, just north of the fence, is unmarked.

2nd Summit   **91 WAUN OER**
                     670m   **785147**
                     Carries a trig pillar.

From the car park, follow the road north for about 400m, go over the stile crossing the fence and bear left onto the ascending path. Continue beside the wall, cross the gravel track and pass beneath the power lines. The path, tenuous at times, slowly moves away from the wall and leads up the long broken flank of the ridge where there is an absence of prominent landmarks. Ascend to the crest, the far side of which is afforested, turn left beside the fence and follow it to the first summit, Mynydd Ceiswyn. Continue east beside the fence, pass through the gate and follow the fence to the second summit, Waun Oer.

To return, head just south of west, drop down the long tussocky slope and cross the stream to the wall corner. Pass the sheepfold, follow the path beside the wall and descend to the gravel track which comes into view. Turn left to the junction, turn right onto the path and walk back to the car park.

ROUTE 64

A demanding walk into a territory removed from time.

Group	Dyfi Forest
Number of summits	1
Time required	3¾ hours
Map	O.S. 1:25 000 Outdoor Leisure Sheet 23
Start	At 677069 — Pandy Square, Abergynolwyn
Parking	Limited parking in the square
Nearest centre	Tywyn (12km)

The Summit 95 TARREN Y GESAIL
667m   **710059**
The trig pillar and the stone shelter are to the west of the true summit which is unmarked.

From the square, take the steep quarry road and pass through the gates. Keep right at the fork, drop down along the track to Bryneglwys Quarry (see p.124) and pass through more gates. Turn left onto the waymarked path and progress through the plantation. Pass beneath the ramp, go through the gate and follow the path to the far corner of the forestry block. Turn left and at the next corner, pass through the gate, turn left again and head upslope beside the fence. Approaching the ridge crest, bear right and make the long pull to the summit.

Return by the same route.

ROUTE 65

Discovers the hidden charisma of Gwynedd. For experienced walkers.

Group	Dyfi Forest
Number of summits	2
Time required	3¾ hours
Map	O.S. 1:25 000 Outdoor Leisure Sheet 23
Start	At 677069 — Pandy Square, Abergynolwyn
Parking	Limited parking in the square
Nearest centre	Tywyn (12km)

1st Summit **117 TARREN HENDRE**
634m   **682041**
Marked by a cairn. The conspicuous mound to the south-east is probably the remains of a Bronze Age round barrow.

2nd Summit **182 MYNYDD TAN Y COED**
491m   **667048**
Marked by a cairn.

From the square, take the steep quarry road and pass through the gates. Keep right at the fork, drop down along the track to Bryneglwys Quarry* and pass through more gates. Cross the bridge towards the forest and about 50m short of the gate, turn left onto the path, pass the spoil heaps and enter the plantation. Pass through the gaps in the fence and the wall, bear right at the fork and head upslope to the saddle (the way the Aberdyfi-bound packhorses would have toiled from Bryneglwys Quarry). Cross the stile, turn right and ascend to Tarren Hendre, the first summit. From here, head north-west, drop down beside the fence and pass through the gate crossing the track. Bear left beside the rising fence, pass through the gate and continue forward. On reaching the disintegrated fence, bear left and follow it to the second summit, Mynydd Tan y Coed.

To return, descend north beside the fence, aim for the sheepfold and pick up the track. Pass through the gate to the forest edge, turn left and drop down sharply beside the fence. After 150m, cross the stile into the forest, follow the path to the access road and bear left. Cross the track of the Tal y Llyn Railway,** turn right onto the B4405 and walk back to Abergynolwyn.

* Bryneglwys Quarry, the slate from which is on the roof of Westminster Hall, was first worked on a small scale in the 1830s. It was the lifeline of Abergynolwyn village for nearly a century. In 1865, the quarry's take-off point, it was linked to the mainline at Tywyn by the Tal y Llyn Railway, the slate having previously been humped over mountain tracks by packhorse to Aberdyfi. Employing over 300 men, the quarry's peak of production was reached in 1875 but, in the early 1880s, the slate industry entered a period of depression and most quarries began feeling the pinch. At the turn of the century, however, there was a sudden demand for slate from the smaller concerns such as Bryneglwys, caused mainly by the bitter strike at the great Penrhyn Quarry. (The strike started in December 1900 and was eventually settled in November 1903, the longest dispute in the history of industrial relations. It contributed appreciably to the introduction of the roofing tile in Britain and the decline of the slate industry in Wales.) Threatened by closure in 1909, Bryneglwys and the Railway were bought by Henry Haydn Jones (local landowner, elected Liberal MP for Merioneth in 1911 and knighted in 1937). He revitalised the quarry, restoring confidence in the community but, as time went by, the problem of finding markets for the slate proved too much. In 1947, with the work-force reduced to six, Bryneglwys was finally abandoned and left to the mercy of the elements.

** The Tal y Llyn Railway was opened in 1865 by the Manchester based cotton firm, McConnel's, a year earlier having bought the quarry with plans to expand it. In October 1866, the railway was made public from Tywyn to Abergynolwyn, the stretch from there to the quarry remaining for slate traffic use only. The derivation of the railway's name is unclear — there appears to have been no intention of extending the line further inland towards Tal y Llyn Lake. When Sir Henry Haydn Jones died in 1950, the railway seemed fated but the Tal y Llyn Railway Preservation Society was formed and the line was saved. The

Society was the first of its kind in the world to operate a railway. Since 1951, its members have relaid the track, strengthened the bridges and rebuilt the stations.

ROUTE 66

Explores part of the great moorland dome from which three principal rivers, including the Severn, the longest in the United Kingdom, have their source. For experienced walkers.

Group	Pumlumon
Number of summits	3
Time required	4½ hours
Map	O.S. 1:50 000 Landranger Sheet 135
Start	At 797840 — Eisteddfa Gurig Farmhouse-Cafe
Parking	Parking area at the cafe (fee)
Nearest centre	Llanidloes (20km)

1st Summit **51 PEN PUMLUMON FAWR**
752m 789869

Carries three ancient burial cairns. The largest has been mutilated by the incorporation of a shelter and construction of a trig pillar.

2nd Summit **62 PEN PUMLUMON LLYGAD BYCHAN**
727m 799871

Not named on the map. The summit, marked by a cairn, coincides with the Dyfed-Powys county boundary.

3rd Summit **57 PEN PUMLUMON ARWYSTLI**
741m 815878

Carries the remains of three ancient burial cairns.

Cross the stile, pass through the farmyard and follow the track. Keep right at the fork, progress to the remains of Pumlumon Lead Mine (closed in 1895) and at the culvert, turn left. Pick up the path, cross the moor and ascend to Pen Pumlumon Fawr, the first summit. Head east beside the fence to the second summit, Pen Pumlumon Llygad Bychan. Then continue further east to the junction, cross the stile and follow the rising fence to the third and final summit, Pen Pumlumon Arwystli.

To return, cross the stile at the junction and descend south-east beside the forestry perimeter fence which, lower down, crosses a stream (a headwater of the Severn). Keep beside the fence, ascend to the track and turn right to the old Nantiago Lead Mine (dormant since 1920). Bear right at the fork, drop down beside the infant Wye and pass the sheepfolds. After about 400m, turn right onto the gravel track, cross the Wye and pass the river gauging station. Where the track bends right, turn left to the junction, cross the stile and turn right onto the traversing path. Pass through the fence gap, turn left and ascend to the saddle where the A44 comes into view. Descend to the gate, turn right and walk back to the cafe.

ROUTE 67

An escape from the inevitable strains of modern society and culture. Can be attempted by fit novice walkers.

Group	Pumlumon
Number of summits	2
Time required	3¼ hours
Map	O.S. 1:50 000 Landranger Sheet 135
Start	At 797840 — Eisteddfa Gurig Farmhouse-Cafe
Parking	Parking area at the cafe (fee)
Nearest centre	Llanidloes (20km)

1st Summit **81 Y GARN**
684m   **775851**
Carries an ancient burial cairn mutilated by the construction of a shelter.

2nd Summit **162 DRYBEDD**
566m   **772833**
Marked by a cairn.

Cross the stile, pass through the farmyard and follow the track. Bear left at the fork, pass through the gates and progress upslope. Where the track crosses the stream, continue forward, follow the vestigial track to the plantation edge and turn right beside the fence. At the second junction, turn left, continue beside the fence and ascend to the first summit, Y Garn. Drop down south-west, follow the fence to the track and pass through the gate. Turn right, ascend to the junction and turn left to the fence corner. Then continue forward along the ridge crest to Drybedd, the second summit.

To return, drop down due east to the forest corner and turn left beside the perimeter fence. After about 900m, just past the junction, turn right, pick up the track and walk back to the cafe.

ROUTE 68

A taste of tranquillity without venturing far from civilisation. In mist, the proficient use of map and compass will be essential.

Group	Pumlumon
Number of summits	1
Time required	2½ hours
Map	O.S. 1:50 000 Landranger Sheet 135
Start	At 756862 — Nant y Moch Reservoir* car park
Parking	Car park at the start
Nearest centre	Aberystwyth (24km)

The Summit 179 DISGWYLFA FAWR
         507m   **737847**

Crowned by an ancient sepulchral mound surmounted by a modern cairn. In 1937, an excavation of the mound unearthed a canoe-shaped dug-out tree trunk containing a cremation and a small flint chip. Outside the trunk, a lugged Irish type food vessel associated with the burial was recovered.

From the car park, cross the dam, go over the cattlegrid and follow the road. At the next grid, turn left beside the forest edge, cross the stile in the fence and follow the path. After 30m, keep left at the fork, progress through the forest and pass through the fence gap. Continue forward, pick up the path and drop down into the featureless valley. After about 800m, where the path bends right, bear left to the fence gap, cross the stream and climb the long tussocky slope to the summit.

Return by the same route.

* Nant y Moch Reservoir was built between 1957 and 1960 to provide water for the power stations incorporated in the CEGB's Rheidol Hydro-Electric Scheme. The huge buttress-type dam interrupts and regulates the headwaters of the Afon Rheidol, one of Britain's fastest flowing rivers. The Scheme commenced operations in December 1961. It was officially opened in July

1964 by Mr R. A. Cooper, Board Member for Operations and Personnel.

ROUTE 69
Crosses wild and devastating moorland. Not for the beginner.

Group	Cwmdeuddwr
Number of summits	1
Time required	3 hours
Map	O.S. 1:50 000 Landranger Sheet 147
Start	At 836555 — the road-track junction near Llannerch Yrfa smallholding
Parking	Limited roadside at the junction
Nearest centre	Llanwrtyd Wells (11km)

The Summit 112 DRYGARN FAWR
645m   **863584**

Carries two of the finest cairns in Wales. About 500m apart, the cairns were raised in prehistoric times as memorials to the dead. The summit cairn was used during the mid-nineteenth century by the Ordnance Survey as a triangulation station. In 1894, as a mark of respect to the dead ancient Britons they commemorate, both cairns were rebuilt to their present appearance by the Birmingham Corporation — they coincide with the limit of the Elan reservoirs' 18 350ha gathering ground (see p.131).

From the junction, follow the track, pass through the gate and progress into the forest. Bear right at the fork to the forest edge, pass through the gate and turn left onto the path where shortly, on the distant skyline, the summit cairn can just be picked out. Keep to the path, tenuous at times, traverse the moor and ascend to the cairn.

Return by the same route.

ROUTE 70

An unrivalled excursion across one of the few undoubted wildernesses left in Britain. Do not attempt unless highly competent with map and compass.

Group	Cwmdeuddwr
Number of summits	2
Time required	5 hours
Map	O.S. 1:50 000 Landranger Sheet 147
Start	At 900616 — Llannerch y Cawr car park
Parking	Car park at the start
Nearest centre	Rhayader (11km)

1st Summit **139 GORLLWYN**
613m **918590**
Carries an ancient burial cairn mutilated by the incorporation of a shelter and construction of a trig pillar.

2nd Summit **149 Y GAMRIW**
604m **943612**
Crowned by the largest Bronze Age summit cairn in Wales. It has been mutilated by the incorporation of a shepherds' shelter.

From the car park, drop down past the telephone box and cross the bridge spanning the river, the Afon Claerwen. Bear right at the fork and after 150m, pass through the gate, follow the track and progress to the U-turn. At this point, continue forward, pass the cataract and follow the tenuous path into the rising valley which is devoid of distinct landmarks. After about 1km, turn left off the path and ascend due east where the first of a line of small concrete pillars soon comes into view, as does the Gorllwyn cairn on the eastern skyline. (The pillars delineate the boundary of the watershed purchased in 1893 by the Birmingham Corporation for the Elan Reservoir Scheme.)* Follow the pillars which lead across the supreme moorland wilderness to the cairn. Then head north-east and continue to follow the pillars into an otherwise featureless landscape. Aim for the key cairn which eventually appears, turn right and traverse more harsh ground to the second summit, Y Gamriw.

To return, go back to the key cairn and follow the pillars back west. After about 350m, near a pillar, turn right onto the faint traversing path, drop down steadily to the fence corner and cross the stream towards the tree-line. Turn left onto the track, pass through the gates and walk back to the car park.

* The Scheme is one of the most remarkable civil engineering projects ever undertaken in Wales. It was designed by the distinguished Victorian railway engineer James Mansergh to supply water to Birmingham. Construction work commenced in 1893 and at the height of the activity over 5000 men were employed. The Scheme was officially opened in July 1904 by King Edward VII. The huge Claerwen Reservoir was built later, between 1946 and 1952, almost doubling Birmingham's water supply. It was officially opened in October 1952 by the Queen.

ROUTE 71

A worthwhile trip through gentle country. Suitable for family groups with older children.

Group	Cwmdeuddwr
Number of summits	1
Time required	2¼ hours
Map	O.S. 1:50 000 Landranger Sheet 147
Start	At 001591 — the layby and telephone box near Cefn y Maes Farmhouse
Parking	Layby at the start
Nearest centre	Llandrindod Wells (9km)

The Summit 173 DRUM DDU
       537m   **970603**
       Carries an ancient burial cairn mutilated by the incorporation of a shelter.

From the layby, follow the road north and at the crossroads, continue forward. On reaching Blaenglynolwyn Farm, mount the track, cross the cattle grid to the junction and keep left where the elongated summit ridge soon comes into view. Follow the track across the rising grassland and on gaining the ridge, turn right to the cairn.

Return by the same route.

ROUTE 72

A magnificent journey which may stir the emotions. For experienced walkers.

A stretch of the walk overlooks the upper Harley Valley which is used periodically for ammunition testing. When firing is in progress, red warning flags are flown on all approaches to the firing area and access to that part of the valley, encircled with danger signs, is prohibited. The route described presents no danger to those who use it.

Group	Radnor Forest
Number of summits	4
Time required	4¾ hours
Map	O.S. 1:50 000 Landranger Sheet 148
Start	At 212609 — Mutton Dingle, New Radnor
Parking	Roadside in the village
Nearest centre	Kington (10km)

1st Summit **152 WHIMBLE**
599m **205626**
The area's most distinctive hill. The summit carries an ancient sepulchral mound surmounted by a modern cairn.

2nd Summit **141 BACHE HILL**
610m **214636**
Carries an ancient sepulchral mound surmounted by a trig pillar.

3rd Summit **108 BLACK MIXEN**
650m **196643**
Carries an ancient sepulchral mound surmounted by a trig pillar.. The transmitter station is owned by the Dyfed-Powys Police Authority which is responsible for the largest area in England and Wales. The present mast and buildings were erected between 1985 and 1987 when the site was redeveloped.

4th Summit   101 GREAT RHOS
660m   182639
Carries a trig pillar.

Take the lane (Mutton Dingle) to the forest edge, bear left at the fork and follow the track. Pass through the gate, continue beside the fence and ascend to the first summit, Whimble. Drop down north-east to the barn, pass through the gates and follow the track. Keep right at the fork and just past the second gate, turn left. Ascend the heather slope and after 100m, turn left onto the vestigial track to the second summit, Bache Hill. Head north to the tree-line, pass through the gate and continue beside the perimeter fence. Pass through more gates, cross the stile in the fence and turn left onto the access road to the third summit, Black Mixen. From the transmitter station, head due west, pass the obsolete telegraph pole and turn right onto the track to the head of the Harley Valley (named after the Harleys* and commonly, but confusingly, known as the Harley Dingle). At the forest edge, turn left beside the fence, continue to the corner and turn right. At the junction, turn left away from the forest, follow the track beside the fence and at the fork, where the fence veers right, bear left. Then continue along the track which passes within 100m of the Great Rhos trig pillar.

To return, head due south to the fence, turn left and after about 200m, near the danger sign, pass through the gate. Bear right onto the track and after about 300m, bear left at the fork, pass to the west of another danger sign and at the next fork, bear left again. Drop down along the path, pass through the gate and continue downslope with the fence to the left. The path passes a third danger sign and leads to a single handrail bridge. Cross the bridge, turn right and pass through the gate. Turn left, cross the culvert and pass through more gates. Drop down along the metalled roadway, Newgate Lane, turn left onto Church Street and walk back to Mutton Dingle.

* The Harleys, a family of eminent statesmen, the most famous of whom was Robert, were once associated with the parliamentary representation of the Radnor Boroughs. The son of Colonel Sir Edward Harley, Robert was the parliamentary

member for the Radnor Boroughs from 1690 to 1711. In 1701, he was elected Speaker of the House of Commons and in 1711, was elevated to the peerage as Baron Harley of Wigmore and Earl of Oxford and Mortimer. In 1713, as Queen Anne's Chief Minister, he negotiated the Treaty of Utrecht in which Britain received Gibraltar from Spain and the Protestant succession of the Hanoverians was acknowledged. He died in May 1724. His only son, Edward, was born in 1689 and succeeded his father as the second Earl of Oxford, the last of the Harleys to represent the County or Boroughs of Radnor. He died in 1741 and was buried in Westminster Abbey.

ROUTE 73

A picturesque walk but with a stiff pull to the summit.

Group	Radnor Forest
Number of summits	1
Time required	2 hours
Map	O.S. 1:50 000 Landranger Sheet 148
Start	At 139629 — Llandegla Church
Parking	Limited roadside in the hamlet
Nearest centre	Llandrindod Wells (11km)

The Summit 180 COWLOD
502m   **161635**
The highest point is unmarked.

Opposite the church, pass through the gate and follow the lane (Tynllan Lane). Pass the farmhouse, Vronlace, keep left at the fork and drop down beside the edge of the deciduous wood to the gate. Cross the stream, mount the hillside and ascend to the summit.

Return by the same route.

ROUTE 74

Stringent action centred on the pass, Bwlch Giedd, the only depression in the spectacular east-facing Mynydd Du escarpment. For experienced walkers.

Group	Carmarthen Fan
Number of summits	3
Time required	3¾ hours
Map	O.S. 1:25 000 Outdoor Leisure Sheet 12
Start	At 855223 — the unmetalled parking area on the west side of the Trecastle-Tafarn y Garreg road
Parking	Small parking area at the start
Nearest centre	Sennybridge (13km)

1st Summit **36 FAN BRYCHEINIOG**
·802m   **825217**
One of the great summit viewpoints of Wales. Carries a trig pillar and a stone shelter.

2nd Summit **54 BANNAU SHIR GÂR**
749m   **811218**
Usually known by its scarp name rather than Picws Du, the peak name. The pile of stones at the summit are likely to be the remains of a Bronze Age burial cairn.

3rd Summit **48 FAN HIR**
760m   **830209**
The highest point, just south of the boulders, is unmarked.

From the parking area, head south-west, pick up the path and make headway across the moor where there are numerous tributary streams. Pass the glacial lake, Llyn y Fan Fawr,* mount the escarpment path (known as the 'Staircase') and ascend to the pass, Bwlch Giedd. Then continue north-west and follow the path to Fan Brycheiniog, the first summit. Descend due west to the col, Bwlch Blaen Twrch, cross the stream onto the path and climb sharply to the second summit, Bannau Shir Gâr. From here, drop back down to the col, head roughly south-east and ascend back to Bwlch Giedd. Now head south and follow the rising scarp crest to Fan Hir, the third and final summit.

To return, go back to Bwlch Giedd, descend the Staircase and walk back to the parking area.

* Llyn y Fan Fawr, trapped in a wild and dramatic location, was formed thousands of years ago by the passage of a glacier. The source of the Tawe and a feeder of the Usk, the lake was created when the retreating ice deposited lateral and terminal moraines of boulder clay which impeded the escaping water. South of the lake, at the foot of the long Fan Hir stretch of the scarp, is another Ice Age feature, an extended bank of sandstone blocks which tumbled with the plunging ice.

ROUTE 75
Faces a formidable terrain. A hard circuit.

Group	Carmarthen Fan
Number of summits	5
Time required	5½ hours
Map	O.S. 1:25 000 Outdoor Leisure Sheet 12
Start	At 730192 — the viewpoint car park on the east side of the A4069
Parking	Car park at the start
Nearest centre	Llandeilo (15km)

1st Summit **167 CEFN Y CYLCHAU**
556m   **757197**
The highest point, near the boulder, is unmarked.

2nd Summit **159 CARREG YR OGOF**
585m   **777214**
Carries a trig pillar.

3rd Summit **115 GARREG LAS**
635m   **777203**
A remote and barren outpost. Carries two ancient burial cairns.

4th Summit **151 FOEL FRAITH**
602m   **756182**
Marked by a cairn.

5th Summit **134 GARREG LWYD**
619m   **740179**
Carries an ancient burial cairn once of immense proportions, now mutilated by the incorporation of shelters. A trig pillar stands bewildered among the scattered remains.

From the car park, head south along the road and after 80m, turn left onto the grassy path. After about 350m, where the path bends gently right, continue forward, cross the sodden terrain and pass the cataract falling on the Afon Clydach. Continue east beside the tributary stream and after 300m, where the stream veers right, bear left across the rising grassland, thereby striking roughly north-east. Cross the boulder field, continue upslope and ascend to the silhouetted boulder at the first summit, Cefn y Cylchau. Keep north-east and drop down sharply to the floor of the deep valley, Cwm Sawdde Fechan. Cross the stream, continue north-east and make the toilsome ascent to the second summit, Carreg yr Ogof. From here, head due south to Garreg Las, the third summit, continue south into the wilderness of stone and pass the handsome shepherds' cairn, set up on a rock platform. Persevere across the punishing terrain, slowly move right and drop down the ridge crest to the unmistakable tarn, Blaenllynfell. Then ascend due west to the penultimate summit, Foel Fraith. Now head just south of west and cross the bleak moorland waste to Garreg Lwyd, the fifth and final summit.

To return, head north-west and pass the upright marker stone where the A4069 comes into view. Aim for the building, a toilet block, turn right onto the road and walk back to the car park.

ROUTE 76

A short patrol over featureless grassland. Ideal for familiarising older children with basic navigation techniques.

Group	Carmarthen Fan
Number of summits	1
Time required	¾ hour
Map	O.S. 1:25 000 Outdoor Leisure Sheet 12
Start	At 855223 — the unmetalled parking area on the west side of the Trecastle-Tafarn y Garreg road
Parking	Small parking area at the start
Nearest centre	Sennybridge (13km)

The Summit 156 MOEL FEITY
          591m   848230
          The cairn is about 100m north-west of the true summit which is unmarked.

From the parking area, head north-west, pick up the rising vestigial track and progress upslope. Where the track peters out, keep north-west and continue to the summit.

Return by the same route.

ROUTE 77
Short and easy with interesting views.

Group	Carmarthen Fan
Number of summits	1
Time required	1 hour
Map	O.S. 1:25 000 Outdoor Leisure Sheet 12
Start	At 820271 — Pont ar Wysg car park
Parking	Car park at the start
Nearest centre	Sennybridge (12km)

The Summit 195 FOEL DARW
    424m   **825258**
    Carries a small concrete pillar — a marker
    delineating the limit of the Usk Reservoir
    catchment area.

To the rear of the car park, cross the stile next to the gate and follow the vestigial track beside the forest edge. After about 350m, cross the stile in the fence, turn left and follow the path. Approaching level ground, bear right and ascend to the hilltop.

Return by the same route.

ROUTE 78

Attains a 700m summit with relatively little effort. Ideal for introducing fit older children to hill walking.

Group	Fforest Fawr
Number of summits	1
Time required	1½ hours
Map	O.S. 1:25 000 Outdoor Leisure Sheet 11
Start	At 982202 — the car park opposite the Storey Arms*
Parking	Car park at the start
Nearest centre	Brecon (13km)

The Summit 59 FAN FAWR
        734m   **969193**
        Marked by a cairn.

To the rear of the car park, cross the stile next to the gate, continue forward and pick up the path beside the stream. Where the incline of the slope steepens, the path crosses the stream and beyond the soggy plateau, where it is visible and firmly established, ascends the grassy curving shoulder to the summit.

Return by the same route.

* The Storey Arms, once a cafe and for many years a youth hostel, was never an inn despite its name. Now an outdoor pursuits centre owned by South Glamorgan County Council, its name originates from the Storey Arms Inn, an old coaching house which once stood nearby but closed about 1900.

ROUTE 79

Penetrates the bleak moorland expanse of the privately owned Cnewr Estate where public access is not freely available. The slopes are toilsome; do not attempt unless in good shape.

Route access is using a permitted way created by an informal agreement between the landowners and the Brecon Beacons National Park Committee. Nevertheless, organised groups intending to use the way must first inform the National Park Office at Glamorgan Street, Brecon, LD3 7DP. Access is not allowed during the lambing season between 15th April and 10th May, or during the hours of darkness.

Group	Fforest Fawr
Number of summits	2
Time required	4¼ hours
Map	O.S. 1:25 000 Outdoor Leisure Sheet 11
Start	At 923191 — the small parking area near Maen Llia*
Parking	Small parking area at the start
Nearest centre	Sennybridge (11km)

1st Summit 96 FAN NEDD
663m 913184
Carries a trig pillar and a stone shelter.

2nd Summit 64 FAN GYHIRYCH
725m 880190
Carries a trig pillar.

From the parking area, follow the road south for 100m (about 200m less than the map suggests), go over the stile crossing the fence (the start of the permitted way) and pass through the wall gap. Then head south-west and climb the featureless hillside to Fan Nedd, the first summit. From here, head north-west and drop down the long sweeping slope to the fence and wall junctions at the saddle, Bwlch y Duwynt. Keep to the left of the gate, pass through the wall gap and bear left across the rising grassland. Pass through the fence gate, turn left onto the Estate road and in time, where the road levels out, turn right to the second summit, Fan Gyhirych.

To return, go back to Bwlch y Duwynt but do not be tempted here to follow the wall and fence leading east to the road. To comply with the agreed route, it is necessary to return via Fan Nedd summit.

* Maen Llia, the huge standing stone often associated with the nearby Roman road, Sarn Helen (see p.146), was doubtless raised in Neolithic times long before the Romans came this way. Pointing in a north-south direction, its probable purpose was to show that a way existed over the high pass connecting the Senni and Llia Valleys.

ROUTE 80

A peerless walk on silent hills. In mist, the proficient use of map and compass will be essential.

Group	Fforest Fawr
Number of summits	2
Time required	2½ hours
Map	O.S. 1:25 000 Outdoor Leisure Sheet 11
Start	At 927164 — Blaen Llia car park-picnic site
Parking	Car park at the start
Nearest centre	Hirwaun (13km)

1st Summit 119 FAN LLIA
632m   938186
Marked by a cairn.

2nd Summit 137 FAN DRINGARTH
617m   940192
The highest point is unmarked.

From the car park, cross the Afon Llia at the ford, turn left and cross the stile. Continue forward and after 100m, cross the stile in the fence, turn right and ascend to the ridge crest. Turn left, continue upslope and progress to the conspicuous cairn (a primitive burial monument). Then follow the faint path to Fan Llia, the first summit. Keep to the path and continue further north to Fan Dringarth, the second summit.

To return, drop down due west and about 500m short of the road, turn left onto the track, the Sarn Helen.* Bear left onto the road (a metalled stretch of the Sarn) and walk back to the car park.

* Sarn Helen, the longest Roman road in Wales, may take its name from the Segontian wife of the self-styled Emperor, Magnus Maximus. The road runs intermittently from the Conwy Valley in the north to Neath in the south. A few stretches, now with metalled surfaces, can be used by cars. Maximus, a soldier

of Spanish origin, declared himself ruler of the Western Empire in 383 after a victory over the Picts. Five years later, he marched on Rome to lay claim to the Imperial throne but was captured and executed by the Emperor Theodosius.

ROUTE 81

Where nature is still the master. One stiff slope. Ideal for fit novice walkers.

Group	Fforest Fawr
Number of summits	2
Time required	2 hours
Map	O.S. 1:25 000 Outdoor Leisure Sheet 11
Start	At 971222 — the layby-picnic site on the west side of the A470
Parking	Layby at the start
Nearest centre	Brecon (10km)

1st Summit	**122 CRAIG CERRIG GLEISIAD**	
	629m	**960217**
	Marked by a cairn.	

2nd Summit	**123 FAN FRYNYCH**	
	629m	**957227**
	Carries a trig pillar.	

To the rear of the picnic site, turn left beside the wall, follow the path and cross the stile next to the gate. Then make the toilsome ascent beside the fence to the first summit, Craig Cerrig Gleisiad. Continue beside the fence, pass through the gate to enter the nature reserve* and ascend along the stony track. Where the track levels out, bear left and proceed the short distance to the second summit, Fan Frynych.

To return, rejoin the track, turn left and drop down to the U-turn. Cross the stile, follow the path and continue downslope. On reaching the second reserve information board, turn left and follow the path back to the layby.

* Craig Cerrig Gleisiad National Nature Reserve, established in 1958, safeguards an area of wild natural beauty which is of prime concern to nature conservation. The brooding north-facing crags of the reserve, eroded by the movement of ice, provide one of the most southerly environments in Britain for the rare arctic-alpine plants left by the receding glaciers, including

cowberry, dovedale moss, green spleenwort and purple saxifrage. The crags are a breeding place for buzzards, kestrels, ravens and ring ouzels.

To visit areas within the reserve away from the public rights of way, permission must be sought from the Nature Conservancy Council, Plas Gogerddan, Aberystwyth, Dyfed, SY23 3EE.

ROUTE 82

An effortless walk from the Brecon Beacons Mountain Centre. *

Group	Fforest Fawr
Number of summits	1
Time required	1¼ hours
Map	O.S. 1:25 000 Outdoor Leisure Sheet 11
Start	At 977262 — Brecon Beacons Mountain Centre
Parking	Car park at the start (fee)
Nearest centre	Brecon (8km)

The Summit 200 TWYN Y GAER
367m   **989280**

An ancient British settlement, the defences of which, although comparatively simple, can still be picked out. Such settlements, each with their own characteristics, were constructed mainly during the second half of the final millennium BC, usually on hilltop terrain above fertile land. They are frequently referred to as 'hill forts' but all available evidence favours the view that no serious conflict took place around them until Roman times. The defences, single or multiple timber-laced earth ramparts, ditches and stone walls, together with cleverly engineered entrances, served primarily as a deterrent to would-be intruders.

From the car park entrance, turn right to the junction, continue forward and follow the track across the common (named after St Illtud).** After about 900m, bear left at the fork, cross the roads and ascend to the trig pillar.

Return by the same route.

* The Centre was opened to fulfil the enjoyment of the Park's thousands of visitors. It is administered by the National Park Committee. A magnificent viewpoint, its facilities include an information desk, a bookshop, a buffet, a picnic terrace and a first aid room. (There are facilities for the disabled.) The Centre

was officially opened in June 1966 by the Rt. Hon. Cledwyn Hughes (now Lord Penrhos), Secretary of State for Wales, 1966-68.

** St Illtud was born about 450 in Brittany. One of the most respected Christian leaders of his time, he introduced Celtic monasticism to Britain from the continent. He was the founder of several religious institutions in South Wales including the great school of divinity and missionary centre at Llantwit Major. Here, many of the famous were educated including: St David, patron saint of Wales; St Samson of Dol, patron saint of Caldey Island where Illtud founded a monastery; St Gildas, the historian; St Paulinus of Leon; and Maelgwn Gwynedd, great-grandson of the Romano-British chieftain, Cunedda Wledig. Illtud is said to be buried on the common, where he once built a cell, but his remains have never been discovered.

ROUTE 83

A favourite excursion along clearly defined paths. Can be attempted by fit novice walkers.

Group	Brecon Beacons
Number of summits	3
Time required	3¼ hours
Map	O.S. 1:25 000 Outdoor Leisure Sheet 11
Start	At 987198 — Pont ar Daf car park
Parking	Car park at the start
Nearest centre	Brecon (14km)

1st Summit **19 PEN Y FAN**
886m   **012215**

One of the highest mountains of the Old Red Sandstone in the British Isles. The panorama from the summit, as would be expected, is extensive. On a clear day it is possible to pick out the Somerset Hills and the coast of Devon. The summit carries an ancient burial cairn surmounted by a trig pillar.

2nd Summit **21 CORN DU**
873m   **007213**

Carries the remains of an ancient burial cairn, excavated in 1978. The cairn covered a cist which had been robbed, probably in the late nineteenth century and no traces of a burial or artefacts survived. A radio-carbon dating method, first suggested by an American professor in 1946, established an early Bronze Age date for the cairn, about 1800 BC.

3rd Summit **135 Y GURN**
619m   **988215**

The cairn is to the east of the true summit which is unmarked.

To the south of the car park toilet block, take the path between the conifers, pass through the gate and cross the stream, the Blaen Taf Fawr. Continue along the path, pass the National Trust plaque* and cross the mountainside to the pass, Bwlch

Duwynt, where the landscape to the east is revealed. Then head north-east, keep to the level path and after about 600m, at the junction, continue forward to Pen y Fan, the first summit. Go back to the junction, keep right and ascend to the second summit, Corn Du. Drop down north-west and follow the path along the scarp edge. After about 500m, bear left at the fork, pass the Tommy Jones obelisk** and continue downslope. Cross the junction to the fence, turn left and follow the fence to the third and final summit, Y Gurn.

To return, continue beside the fence, pick up the path ascending from the left and cross the stile. Drop down to the A470, turn left and walk back to the car park.

* The plaque commemorates the gift of the Brecon Beacons to the National Trust by the Eagle Star Insurance Company in 1965.

** The obelisk commemorates a five-year-old boy who died in August 1900. The son of a Rhondda miner, Tommy lost his way near Cwm Llwch Farmhouse while visiting his grandparents, starting a twenty-nine day search which aroused nationwide concern. His body was found by a Mr and Mrs Hamer of Castell Madog near Brecon at the spot marked by the obelisk — a dream guiding them to the precise location. Tommy had died from exhaustion and exposure, but how a small boy managed to climb so high remains a mystery. The obelisk, a useful landmark in misty conditions, was paid for by the proceeds of a memorial fund started when the jurors at the boy's inquest waived their fees.

ROUTE 84

Infiltrates fine walking country. Not for the beginner.

Group	Brecon Beacons
Number of summits	3
Time required	4 hours
Map	O.S. 1:25 000 Outdoor Leisure Sheet 11
Start	At 037237 — the road-track junction at the entrance to Cwm Cynwyn Farm
Parking	Limited roadside at the junction
Nearest centre	Brecon (5km)

1st Summit   39 CRIBYN
795m   **023213**
Sometimes called 'the Welsh Matterhorn', a tribute more closely linked with Cnicht in the Moelwyni. The low pile of stones at the summit are probably the remains of an ancient burial cairn.

2nd Summit   66 FAN Y BIG
719m   **036206**
Characterised by the 'diving board', a much photographed rock platform which projects from the summit over the steep scarp.

3rd Summit   61 GWAUN CERRIG LLWYDION
730m   **041196**
A bleak hag-ridden moor known locally as the 'moon country'. The highest point, crossed by the path, is unmarked.

From the junction, take the track leading south (a possible Roman road)* and pass through the gate. Bear right off the track, pick up the path and make headway up the crest of the ridge, Bryn-teg. The path rises steadily, passes a prominent cairn and eventually strikes up the 'nose', the steep north ridge of Cribyn. Ascend to the summit, head south-east and drop down to the 'Roman road' at the pass, Bwlch ar y Fan (better known as the 'Gap'). Cross the road, continue forward and make the sharp pull to Fan y Big, the second summit. Follow the path leading south, merge with the path ascending from the Gap and circle the scarp crest to the third and final summit, Gwaun Cerrig Llwydion.

To return, go back to the Gap, turn right onto the 'Roman road' and walk back to the junction.

* The 'Roman road' crossing the Beacons often evokes curiosity among historians regarding its authenticity. While the road bears certain hallmarks of Roman engineering, it is doubtful that it is Roman in origin. It has been suggested that the road linked the Y Gaer auxiliary fort near Brecon, which was built about AD 80, to areas further south where other Roman garrisons were established. However, this seems unlikely to be the case bearing in mind the route taken later by Sarn Helen (see p.146).

ROUTE 85

A hard trek on melancholic hills. Ideal for the lone pedestrian.

Group	Brecon Beacons
Number of summits	3
Time required	5 hours
Map	O.S. 1:25 000 Outdoor Leisure Sheet 11
Start	At 099197 — the Water Authority car park near Tal-y-bont Reservoir*
Parking	Car park at the start
Nearest centre	Brecon (13km)

1st Summit **106 ALLT LWYD**
654m   **078189**
Marked by a cairn.

2nd Summit **46 WAUN RYDD**
769m   **062206**
Marked by a cairn.

3rd Summit **165 BRYN**
562m   **071226**
The cairn is to the north-east of the true summit which is unmarked.

Opposite the car park, take the forestry road for 50m, cross the stile and follow the track. Bear left to the forest edge, cross the stile at the corner and ascend to the first summit, Allt Lwyd. Head north-west, cross the saddle and climb sharply to the peat moor. Keep north-west, follow the path across the moor and after about 1km, near two small tarns, continue forward to the Waun Rydd summit cairn. From here, drop down due north, pick up the path descending from the left and at the fork, keep right. At the next fork, on level ground, bear right to the third and final summit, Bryn.

To return, head just north of east, descend to the forest edge and pass through the gate. Follow the path into the forest and at the access road, turn left. Bear right at the fork and at the T-junction, turn right. Take the first turning left, pass through the gate at the forest edge and follow the path. Pass through the gate, drop down along the lane and at the crossroads, turn right. At the T-junction near Gethinog Farmhouse, turn right again, continue to the valley road and walk back to the car park.

* Tal-y-bont Reservoir, the haunt of myriads of wildfowl, was created by damming the Afon Caerfanell to supply water to the Newport area. Construction work began in July 1932 and on completion, six years later, the reservoir's capacity was sufficient to provide everyone in the world with a gallon of water each. It was officially opened in June 1939 by Alderman J. R. Wardell, Chairman of Newport Waterworks Committee, 1935-51. In 1975, the reservoir was established as a local nature reserve. Its wide diversity of habitat attracts numerous wildfowl species including the grand winter visitors from Russia and northern Europe, Bewick's and whooper swan.

ROUTE 86

A direct march across desolate moorland. Do not attempt unless competent with map and compass.

Group	Brecon Beacons
Number of summits	1
Time required	2½ hours
Map	O.S. 1:25 000 Outdoor Leisure Sheet 11
Start	At 117133 — about 600m north of Trefil Post Office
Parking	Ample roadside at the start
Nearest centre	Tredegar (4km)

The Summit 136 CEFN YR YSTRAD
       617m   **086137**
       A remote outpost. Carries a trig pillar.

From the road and about 150m north of the pool, drop down across the stream, the Nant Trefil, pick up the faint rising path and make headway across the moor. Where the path peters out, keep just north of west, cross the boulder fields and pass, at some distance, the conspicuous stone (a nineteenth century parish boundary marker, others may be visible). At this point, continue forward, aim for the cairns (primitive burial monuments) and proceed to the trig.

Return by the same route.

ROUTE 87

Away from the region's main tourist spots. Suitable for casual walkers and family groups.

Group	Brecon Beacons
Number of summits	1
Time required	1¼ hours
Map	O.S. 1:25 000 Outdoor Leisure Sheet 11
Start	At 056175 — Torpantau car park
Parking	Car park at the start
Nearest centre	Merthyr Tudful (11km)

The Summit 163 PANT Y CREIGIAU
             565m   **056162**
             Carries a trig pillar.

From the car park entrance, turn right and follow the road. After about 400m, turn left onto the metalled track, bear right at once onto the rutted track and ascend to the summit.

Return by the same route.

ROUTE 88

A possibility for the active senior citizen.

Group	Brecon Beacons
Number of summits	1
Time required	¾ hour
Map	O.S. 1:25 000 Outdoor Leisure Sheet 11
Start	At 109187 — the road-track junction at the entrance to Bwlch y Waun Farm
Parking	Small parking area at the junction
Nearest centre	Brecon (15km)

The Summit 169 TOR Y FOEL
551m   **114194**
Marked by a cairn.

From the junction, an easily followed path climbs direct to the summit.

Return by the same route.

ROUTE 89

A classic ridge walk. An arduous undertaking; do not attempt unless in good shape.

Group	Black Mountains
Number of summits	4
Time required	7 hours
Map	O.S. 1:25 000 Outdoor Leisure Sheet 13
Start	At 277223 — the small parking area below Partrishow Church*
Parking	Parking area at the start
Nearest centre	Crickhowell (9km)

1st Summit **170 CRUG MAWR**
550m   **262226**
Carries a trig pillar.

2nd Summit **104 PEN TWYN MAWR**
658m   **242267**
Marked by a cairn.

3rd Summit **37 PEN Y GADAIR FAWR**
800m   **229287**
Carries an ancient burial cairn.

4th Summit **33 WAUN FACH**
810m   **215299**
Marked by a cairn. The concrete slab is the base of an old trig pillar.

From the parking area, head north past the church and after 500m, just short of the gate, bear left onto the rising track. Pass through the gate, bear left again and follow the path beside the fence. On reaching the wall, turn right onto the faint path and ascend through the bracken. The path slowly bends left, climbs the gentle heather slope and leads to the first summit, Crug Mawr. From here, head north to the forest corner, pick up the ridge path ascending from the left and eventually, at the junction cairn, bear left to Pen Twyn Mawr, the summit the ridge path ignores. Rejoin the path and follow it north to the unmistakable third summit, Pen y Gadair Fawr. Then traverse the long saddle to the fourth and final summit, Waun Fach.

Return by the same route, skirting the summits.

* Partrishow Church is dedicated to the hermit priest, St Issui, who lived in the sixth century. It is best known for its magnificent rood-screen and loft which was erected in the late fifteenth century when the church was extensively restored. The screen, fashioned from Irish oak left in its natural colour, is thought to be the work of an Italian woodcarver employed at nearby Llanthony Priory. A small part of the original church, probably eleventh century, is believed to be contained in the chapel in the west wall of the present building. The chapel has mainly thirteenth century characteristics and possibly held the shrine of the saint. Issui lived in a cell in the dingle below the church near the holy well, Ffynnon Ishow. The well is claimed to possess healing properties. After the unfortunate saint was murdered there, the cell became a place of pilgrimage.

ROUTE 90

Offers excellent panoramic views. For experienced walkers.

Group	Black Mountains
Number of summits	3
Time required	4¼ hours
Map	O.S. 1:25 000 Outdoor Leisure Sheet 13
Start	At 184252 — the layby-picnic site on the west side of the A479
Parking	Layby at the start
Nearest centre	Crickhowell (8km)

1st Summit **97 MYNYDD LLYSIAU**
663m   **207279**
The cairn is to the south-east of the true summit which is unmarked.

2nd Summit **111 PEN TWYN GLAS**
646m   **213257**
Carries two nineteenth century boundary stones, sepulchral in appearance, which once recorded the estate limits of local landowners.

3rd Summit **67 PEN ALLT MAWR**
719m   **206243**
Carries an ancient burial cairn mutilated by the incorporation of a shelter and construction of a trig pillar.

From the layby, follow the road north for about 700m, bear right onto the lane and continue to the staggered crossroads. Bear right onto the ascending track, pass beneath the power lines and at the T-junction, turn right. Cross the cattle grid to the edge of the pine wood, turn left onto the path and pass through the gates. After 150m, near the conifers, turn left onto the grassy path and progress upslope to the wall. Where the wall turns right, continue forward and ascend to the first summit, Mynydd Llysiau. Then head south along the well established ridge path to Pen Twyn Glas, the second summit. The path leads further south to the third and final summit, Pen Allt Mawr.

To return, go back along the path for about 1km where it bends right, turn left and drop down the heather slope to the fence. Turn left, pass through the wall gate and follow the track. Drop down to the farmyard, Pen yr Heol, cross the lane onto the descending track and after 400m, just short of the gate, turn left onto the seldom-used path. On reaching the lane, turn left and walk back to the layby.

ROUTE 91

Along a stretch of the handsome wedge of Old Red Sandstone which overlooks the Wye Valley. An easily managed walk.

Group	Black Mountains
Number of summits	2
Time required	2¼ hours
Map	O.S. 1:25 000 Outdoor Leisure Sheet 13
Start	At 235352 — the head of Gospel Pass*
Parking	Parking area at the start
Nearest centre	Hay on Wye (9km)

1st Summit 78 TWMPA
690m   224350
Also known as Lord Hereford's Knob. The summit is marked by a cairn.

2nd Summit 68 PEN RHOS DIRION
713m   211334
Carries a trig pillar.

From the true head of the pass, mount the rutted track and follow it up the escarpment shoulder to Twmpa, the first summit. Continue along the track, drop down to the grassy col and at the fork, bear right to Pen Rhos Dirion, the second summit.

Return by the same route.

* Gospel Pass, the upper gateway to the Black Mountain's only glacial valley, the Vale of Ewyas, could take its name from legend. This records that St Peter and St Paul crossed the pass to preach the gospel to the Silurian tribesfolk at the request of one of the grandaughters of Cunobelinus, 'King of the Britons', who died in AD 40. In the late twelfth century, however, while preaching and fund raising for the Third Crusade, Giraldus Cambrensis (Gerald of Wales) also crossed the pass and its name is more likely to derive from this. (In 1175, Cambrensis became Archdeacon of Brecon when no more than thirty years of age.)

ROUTE 92

A step into prehistory. Suitable for fit novice walkers.

Group   Black Mountains
Number of summits 2
Time required   2¾ hours
Map   O.S. 1:25 000 Outdoor Leisure Sheet 13
Start   At 234202 — the road junction about 600m west of Llanbedr village centre
Parking   Limited roadside at the junction
Nearest centre   Crickhowell (2km)

1st Summit   **189 CRUG HYWEL**
                        451m   **225207**

The watchtower of Crickhowell. An ancient British settlement occupying the summit of Table Mountain. The settlement is overlooked from the nearby escarpment and shielded by simple bivallate defences, signifying perhaps an early Iron Age construction of about 500 BC. Used intermittently down the centuries, its last inhabitant is said to have been the influential tenth century lawgiver, Hywel (Dda) ap Cadell, King of all Wales outside Morgannwg and grandson of Rhodri Mawr, the only Welsh king to be called Great.

2nd Summit   **72 PEN CERRIG CALCH**
                        701m   **217223**

Carries a trig pillar and the remains of two ancient burial cairns. Formed of Carboniferous age rocks, the summit area is the only remaining part of the South Wales coal basin north of the Usk. The rocks of the landscape can otherwise be assigned to the preceding Devonian period which saw the appearance of the first amphibians.

From the junction, head north along the road for 500m, cross the stile next to the gate and follow the steep track to Perth y Pia (a fifteenth century farmhouse now restored as a bunk house).

Cross the stile, bear right to the tree-lined fence and pass through the gate. Follow the path, continue upslope and cross the traversing track to Crug Hywel, the first summit. Drop down north, pick up the path and ascend through the bracken. The path, clearly defined, climbs steadily up the face of the scarp and leads to Pen Cerrig Calch, the second summit.

To return, go back along the path for about 300m where it bends right, continue forward and drop down just south of east to the block of trees which comes into view. Pass through the wall gate, follow the path and descend to the road. Turn right and walk back to the junction.

ROUTE 93

A ridge walk of quality. Incorporates Wales's easternmost 600m peak. An energetic trip.

Group	Black Mountains
Number of summits	2
Time required	3½ hours
Map	O.S. 1:25 000 Outdoor Leisure Sheet 13
Start	At 266251 — Ffawyddog car park-picnic site
Parking	Car park at the start
Nearest centre	Abergavenny (8km)

1st Summit   **187 Y GARN WEN**
471m   **280255**

A minor summit with a magnificent cairn — a masterpiece of the art of drystone walling. The cairn was built, it is said, about 1900 by a local farmer while waiting to meet a friend from a nearby valley. They would meet there from time to time to exchange sheep that had strayed as well as to gossip. The friend was always late and so the farmer started to build a cairn. Its size and the meticulous way in which it is constructed suggests they were meeting there for some considerable time. Much of the stone used would doubtless have been from the primitive burial site on which the cairn is superimposed.

2nd Summit   **84 CHWAREL Y FAN**
679m   **258294**

Wales's easternmost 600m peak. The summit is marked by a cairn and coincides with the Gwent-Powys county boundary. It is a splendid vantage-point for the Hatterrall Ridge which straddles the England-Wales border and carries Offa's Dyke Path (see p.72).

To the north-east of the car park, pass through the gate, follow the track and progress into the forest. Pass the homestead, Cadwgan, continue to the forest edge and pass through the gate.

Cross the stream, bear left onto the faint path and ascend the laborious heather slope. The path moves slowly away from the forest, crosses the track descending from its corner and leads to the first summit cairn, Y Garn Wen. From here, head north-west, follow the track and ascend to the Bâl Bach junction cairn (where an old packhorse trail crosses the ridge). Bear left, climb to the trig pillar on the Bâl Mawr ridge step and follow the path to Chwarel y Fan, the second summit.

To return, go back to the Bâl Mawr trig and drop down south to the forest edge. Cross the stile to enter the forest, follow the path and pass the cottage, Pen y Cae. Turn left at the T-junction, continue to the fork and bear right to the car park.

ROUTE 94

Short but testing.

Group	Black Mountains
Number of summits	1
Time required	1 hour
Map	O.S. 1:25 000 Outdoor Leisure Sheet 13
Start	At 239373 — the car park near the stone circle
Parking	Car park at the start
Nearest centre	Hay on Wye (7km)

The Summit 86 HAY BLUFF
677m   244366
Also known as Pen y Beacon. The summit carries a trig pillar.

From the car park, follow the path across the common and progress up the escarpment face. Half-way up, the path, pursuing the easier gradient, veers right, climbs to the scarp crest and emerges within view of the trig.

Return by the same route.

ROUTE 95

*Visits one of the most easily attained 600m summits in Wales.
Unsuitable for families with young children.*

Group	Black Mountains
Number of summits	1
Time required	1 hour
Map	O.S. 1:25 000 Outdoor Leisure Sheet 13
Start	At 160283 — the head of Cwm Sorgwm
Parking	Small parking area at the start
Nearest centre	Talgarth (8km)

The Summit 144 MYNYDD TROED
        609m   **165292**
        Carries a trig pillar.

From the parking area, pass through the gate onto the path,
continue forward and ascend to the summit.

Return by the same route.

ROUTE 96

The trade route to the Sugar Loaf. Can be attempted by energetic casual walkers.

Group	Black Mountains
Number of summits	1
Time required	1¾ hours
Map	O.S. 1:25 000 Outdoor Leisure Sheet 13
Start	At 268167 — Llanwenarth car park
Parking	Car park at the start
Nearest centre	Abergavenny (4km)

The Summit 154 MYNYDD PEN Y FAL
596m   **272187**

Better known as the Sugar Loaf because of its resemblance, from certain viewpoints, to a heap of sugar when poured from a bag. In 1936, the hill and surrounding land, an area of 852ha, was given to the National Trust by Viscountess Rhondda. The summit carries a trig pillar.

To the rear of the car park, follow the track to the wall, bear left at the fork and at the next fork, keep right. Cross the traversing paths, progress upslope and ascend to the summit.

Return by the same route.

ROUTE 97

A leisurely stroll. Safe for families with young children.

Group	Black Mountains
Number of summits	1
Time required	¾ hour
Map	O.S. 1:50 000 Landranger Sheet 161
Start	At 263107 — Foxhunter* car park
Parking	Car park at the start
Nearest centre	Blaenafon (3km)

The Summit 166 BLORENGE
         561m   **269118**
         Carries a trig pillar and an ancient burial cairn.

From the east side of the car park, an improving path leads direct to the summit.

Return by the same route.

* Foxhunter, the famous horse from which the car park takes its name, was born in April 1940 in Norfolk. Triumphant in over seventy international competitions, his finest hour came in 1952 at the Helsinki Olympics where he won a gold medal in the Nations Cup team event with Aherlow and Nizefela. (Foxhunter's owner, Sir Harry Llewellyn, was the winner of over 150 international competitions.) The horse died in 1959 and his grave, marked by a memorial plaque, is to the rear of the car park.

ROUTE 98

A placid walk along easily followed tracks.

Group	Black Mountains
Number of summits	1
Time required	1½ hours
Map	O.S. 1:25 000 Outdoor Leisure Sheet 13
Start	At 160283 — the head of Cwm Sorgwm
Parking	Small parking area at the start
Nearest centre	Talgarth (8km)

The Summit 176 MYNYDD LLAN-GORS
         515m   **159266**
         The highest point is unmarked and difficult to
         define.

From the parking area, mount the rutted track, keep left at the
fork and make headway up the shoulder of the hill. On attaining
the crest, bear right at the fork, pass the lone boulder and cross
the track junction. Then bear left and pass between the pools to
the summit.

Return by the same route.

ROUTE 99

Samples a landscape rich in history and legend. Ideal for casual walkers and family groups.

Group	Black Mountains
Number of summits	1
Time required	1½ hours
Map	O.S. 1:25 000 Outdoor Leisure Sheet 13
Start	At 328164 — Skirrid Fawr car park
Parking	Car park at the start
Nearest centre	Abergavenny (3km)

The Summit 183 YSGYRYD FAWR
486m   **331182**

Anglicised as Skirrid Fawr. The summit carries a trig pillar which is surrounded by the foundations of the small medieval Roman Catholic chapel of St Michael, used until the seventeenth century. The foundations, a low undulating bank, cover a rectangular area of about 8m x 6m. The two upright stones in the south side of the bank, between which the path leads to the pillar, are thought to be the remains of the chapel doorway jambs. The local name of the hill, the Holy Mountain, derives from the legend which states that it was created at the time of the Crucifixion. The tale once led people to take soil from its slopes to dig into their own land, confident that their crops would improve. In 1939, the upper 83ha of the hill was given to the National Trust by Major J.A. Herbert, MP.

To the west of the car park, cross the stile onto the path and progress to the corner of the wood. Cross the stile, follow the path into the wood and cross the stile in the wall. Turn right to the fork, bear right (avoiding the eroded path) and continue upslope. On reaching level ground, turn left onto the ascending path and follow it to the trig.

Return by the same route.

ROUTE 100

Locates an oasis of tranquillity but do not be deceived by the summer height.

Group	Black Mountains
Number of summits	1
Time required	2 hours
Map	O.S. 1:25 000 Outdoor Leisure Sheet 13
Start	At 292200 — the car park on the west side of the Betws-Fforest Coal Pit road
Parking	Car park at the start
Nearest centre	Abergavenny (6km)

The Summit 199 BRYN ARW
384m   **301206**
Marked by a cairn.

From the car park, follow the road south to Betws Church, turn left onto the lane and continue along the track. Pass through the gate, bear left onto the sharply rising path and pass the wall corner to the fence. Where the fence turns left, ascend to the summit ridge, turn left onto the faint path and proceed to the cairn.

Return by the same route.

GLOSSARY OF 100 WELSH WORDS

aber .... estuary
afon(ydd) .... river(s)
allt .... cliff, height
aran .... high place

bach .... little, small
bedd .... grave
blaen .... head of, top
bont .... bridge
braich .... arm, spur
bryn .... hill
bwlch .... col, pass, saddle

cadair .... chair
canol .... middle
capel .... chapel
carnedd .... cairn
cau .... hollow
cefn .... ridge
clogwyn .... precipice
cnicht .... knight
coch .... red
coed .... forest, wood
cors .... bog, swamp
craig .... crag
crib .... ridge
croes .... cross
crug .... hillcock
cwm .... cirque, valley
cwta .... short

dôl .... meadow
drws .... door
du, ddu .... black
dŵr .... water

eglwys .... church
eira .... snow
esgair .... ridge

fach .... little, small
fan .... crest, peak
fawr .... big, large
ffordd .... road
foel .... hill, mountain

gadair .... chair
gallt .... slope
garnedd .... cairn
goch .... red
groes .... cross
grug .... heather
gwlyb .... wet
gwynt .... wind

hafod .... summer house
hebog .... hawk
hen .... old
hendre .... winter house
hir .... long

isaf .... lower

llan .... church, parish
llwybr .... path
llyn(nau) .... lake(s)

maen .... stone
maes .... field
mawr .... big, large
melin .... mill

178

moel .... hill	*saeth* .... arrow
mynydd .... mountain	*sarn* .... causeway
	sych .... dry
nant .... brook, stream	*tomen* .... mound
newydd .... new	*traeth* .... shore
	tref .... town
oer .... cold	*trum* .... ridge
ogof ....cave	*twll* .... hole
	tŷ .... house
pant .... hollow, valley	*tyddyn* .... smallholding
parc ....enclosure, field	
pen .... head, top	*uchaf* .... higher, upper
pentre .... village	*un* ....one
plas .... hall, mansion	
poeth .... hot	*waun* .... moor
pont .... bridge	*wen* .... white
porth .... gate	*wrach* .... witch
pwll ....pool	
	y, yr .... the
rhaeadr .... waterfall	*yn* .... in
rhedyn .... bracken	*ynys* .... island
rhiw .... hill, slope	*ysgubor* .... barn
rhos .... moor	
rhyd .... ford	

INDEX